ENDORSEMENTS

This book illustrates the evolution of a successful practice from someone who is creative, disciplined, and client centric. It is a valuable roadmap for anyone willing to work hard and absorb Sal's knowledge and experience, regardless of their stage in their career. For those not in the industry, it is just a great read!

Andrea Wolley

Former Vice President, J.P. Morgan Securities
Former Assistant to Sal Tiano for twenty-seven years

I worked at major retail firms for over twenty-five years before I met Sal Tiano. I managed the municipal bond trading desks at those firms and serviced over fifteen thousand salespeople. However, it was not until I met Sal that I witnessed the true meaning of a financial advisor. His high level of integrity, knowledge, and ethics is rarely matched in the industry. Knowing his clients both on a business and personal relationship is his top priority, and he directs his team to understand that the client base remains our number one focus. I have known Sal for twenty years and I am proud to be part of his team, and, more importantly, a close friend.

Louis J. Ventura

Managing Director, J.P. Morgan Securities

I've been a colleague and friend of Sal Tiano for almost twenty years. Sal has always held himself to the highest standards and has conducted his business in his clients' best interests. He has a relentless desire to improve his practice and to improve the way all of our clients are served, not just his own. If you want to make it to the top of the wealth management profession, Structural Alpha tells you everything you need to know; it's up to you to put Sal's terrific advice into practice.

Adam Frank

Managing Director, Head of Wealth Management, J.P. Morgan Securities

If you want to get somewhere fast, go alone. If you want to go far, take on partners. Sal realized the benefits of creating a team early on in order to best serve clients. This is one example of his ability to anticipate forces and affect positive and meaningful directives. Equally important is the discipline by which he manages and organizes ongoing operations. Human nature has many shy away from change or challenge. True leaders adapt, morph, change, and turn challenge into positive actionable momentum. In my thirty-plus years as an advisor, I was hard-pressed to find a partner that met my high personal standards, until I came to know Sal.

Structural Alpha is a powerful template for any business owner who chooses to rise far above mediocrity and reach the highest level of success.

Louise Armour

Managing Director, Tiano, Armour & Smyth Wealth Managers, J.P. Morgan Securities

I have been a friend and business associate assisting with tax and financial services with Sal Tiano for over fifteen years. In that time, he has proven his strong work ethic, professionalism, integrity, and drive to do/be better. I have watched Sal grow his business into one of the most successful wealth management firms in the country. Sal is a true family man, still finding time to continue his entrepreneurial spirit in the business world.

Howard M. Newburg

CEO & Managing Partner, Newburg & Company, LLP

STRUCTURAL
ALPHA

STRUCTURAL ALPHA

BUILDING & MAINTAINING
AN ELITE WEALTH MANAGEMENT PRACTICE

SAL TIANO

ForbesBooks

Published by ForbesBooks, Charleston, South Carolina.
Member of Advantage Media Group.

ForbesBooks is a registered trademark, and the ForbesBooks colophon is a trademark of Forbes Media, LLC.

Printed in the United States of America.

10 9 8 7 6 5 4 3 2 1

ISBN: 978-1-946633-60-6
LCCN: 2019940106

Cover design by Melanie Cloth.
Layout design by Wesley Strickland.

This publication is designed to provide accurate and authoritative information in regard to the subject matter covered. It is sold with the understanding that the publisher is not engaged in rendering legal, accounting, or other professional services. If legal advice or other expert assistance is required, the services of a competent professional person should be sought.

 Advantage Media Group is proud to be a part of the Tree Neutral® program. Tree Neutral offsets the number of trees consumed in the production and printing of this book by taking proactive steps such as planting trees in direct proportion to the number of trees used to print books. To learn more about Tree Neutral, please visit **www.treeneutral.com**.

Since 1917, the Forbes mission has remained constant. Global Champions of Entrepreneurial Capitalism. ForbesBooks exists to further that aim by bringing the Stories, Passion, and Knowledge of top thought leaders to the forefront. ForbesBooks brings you The Best in Business. To be considered for publication, please visit **www.forbesbooks.com**.

TABLE OF CONTENTS

ACKNOWLEDGMENTS

No book would happen without the help of a great team. I am grateful for my wife Kim for giving up time, resources, and energy by allowing me to work on this book and getting it into your hands. Thirty years ago I told my wife on our second date that I was going to marry her. Kim, thanks for not running away and for sacrificing your own career and believing in me. To my children Salvatore (Tory), Brenna, Will, Nick, and Alexa—you give me five more awesome reasons to get out of bed every morning and put forth my best effort. To my mother Roberta, thank you for teaching me how to speak up for myself and for always putting family above all else. To my role model and father Joe, the best father on earth and most humble man I know. Your optimistic attitude is contagious. Joe and John, my big brothers and best friends: your selfless attitudes are what I admire most about you. Thank you for paving the way for me. To David Nectow, my partner at Pure Hockey: thanks for coming to me with a simple idea and a grand vision. Your work ethic is second to none. To my entire team: John, Louise, Daniel, Jason, Lou, Greg, Nikki, Brenna, Kristin, Julie, Laura, Luther, and Michael: none of this would be possible without you. Your integrity and camaraderie make coming to work easy. And we have a lot of fun together! Thank you for making me look smarter than I really am.

Andrea Wolley, a special shout out to you—my former assistant of over twenty-seven years. Thank you for the care you gave our clients, the long hours you've committed, and your unwavering loyalty to me and your belief in our process. I wouldn't be where I am today without you. Rick Penafiel, my manager for the past twenty years—a real "advisors' manager," very much like a baseball manager who is the first person out of a dugout protecting his players during a brawl. Thank you for your guidance and for believing in me. And for telling me when I'm wrong. And, of course, my business would be nothing without the great clients we've helped over the past thirty years. I have been able to meet some very successful and brilliant people. In fact, partnering with my clients has only taught me to become a better business person, a better advisor, a humbler person. To Barron's, Forbes/SHOOK Research, thank you for helping bring credibility to the industry by acknowledging advisors who truly care about their clients. I've learned so much from attending your conferences.

To Sheila Hopkins: thank you for the countless hours you spent editing this book. You always made yourself available, even around my crazy schedule. You made the process easy and enjoyable and you always stayed positive. Thanks for your professionalism.

To everyone on my Advantage|ForbesBooks team, thank you for all you did to help me bring this book into the world. You made a complex process all the more rewarding.

STRUCTURAL ALPHA

The value we create in our clients' lives from our advice on better ways to structure, organize, and plan for their family needs and goals. It is a systematic, methodical approach that enables you and your team to be indispensable in the eyes of your clients.

FOREWORD

I was just twenty-six years old in 1997 when I started as a supervisor at Bear Stearns. As I walked into the room full of advisors that first day, it took me about three seconds to pinpoint the guy—the person who was the most successful, the most senior, the most admired, the most motivated. Sal Tiano was that guy.

He was younger than nearly everyone else there—in fact, not much older than I was—but he had an aura of leadership and success. He had confidence in who he was and what he did. It's not often that you find somebody who is that confident and has the ability to back it up. When you get that rare combination, you often also get a humble person. And that is Sal.

Even as a young person, Sal was viewed as the mentor for all the other advisors in the room. It didn't matter if they were younger or—more likely—older. He just has this inner core of knowing how to reach people.

This industry is always changing, and Sal is always looking to be at the forefront of where the business is going. For example, years ago, Sal was the first person knocking on management's door saying, "We should be coming up with a fee-based platform for our clients."

What did Sal see in a fee-based platform that others didn't? Sal's focus on his clients is extraordinary, and he realized early on that a fee-based platform would put him on the same side of the table as his client. If the client did well, he would, too. If markets were volatile and clients weren't doing well, he wouldn't do well, either. He knew that clients respect those who are in the trenches with them.

Whenever Sal comes to Boston, I hold an all-hands meeting and ask him to talk about what he's doing today. The room is always at standing-room-only capacity. Everyone wants to hear what Sal is doing, what his challenges are, and how he is building his business by focusing on his clients. He walks them through his current focus, his investment philosophy, some of the investment ideas he likes, and how he is developing his client base. He also talks about what his clients are asking today, where he is getting his ideas, and what research he is following. He then opens the meeting to questions and answers every single one of them. Everyone would love to be able to do what he does the way he does it.

I don't think there is any situation in which Sal is not coaching in some capacity. Whether it is in the office with my other advisors, with his own team as he works with them and teaches them this business, or with his kids, since he coaches nearly all of their sports teams. I don't think there is any aspect of his life where he is not taking advantage of an opportunity to be a coach. He loves it.

Sal is easily the hardest-working person I've ever seen, and he is never satisfied. Every time he sets a goal—and he always tells me what his goals are—he exceeds it and then comes up with a new one.

As a true entrepreneur, he is constantly thinking about his business. He's thinking about his clients. He's thinking about the things he has to do for them. There are people who have jobs, and then there are people who are truly passionate about what they do. Sal is one of those passionate people.

Sal is always learning. He likes to attend senior advisors' meetings to hear what they're doing. This is the best and the worst thing that happens to me, because I have my best advisors getting better, but he comes back with twenty pages of notes, and then he tortures me for about two months. He just learned ten new things, and we'd better be ready to start revamping processes or offering new products that help our advisors service their clients better. But you know what? Sal makes us all better. It's hard work keeping up with him. But his goal is to make everyone else better, and he does.

I have met thousands of advisors in my career, and I don't say this lightly—Sal Tiano is the best financial advisor I have ever known. Period.

And this book is Sal doing what he does best—mentoring, coaching, challenging. It's a book that seeks to bring out the best in the advisors who read it and to provide a platform to help them grow a business by putting their clients first.

Jamie Dimon, chairman and CEO of JPMorgan Chase, once asked everyone in the room whether they had anyone on their team who wasn't afraid to challenge them, who was outspoken, who wasn't afraid to tell them when they thought they were wrong. "If you do," he said. "You should throw everyone else out of the room. That's the person you want to work with."

Sal's my guy. And the hints and tips he provides in his book will make him your guy, too.

Rick Penafiel

Regional Director, J.P. Morgan Securities

INTRODUCTION
WHY I WROTE THIS BOOK

WRITING A BOOK has never been on my radar. I'm a voracious reader, but when it comes to communicating, I prefer the old-fashioned, face-to-face approach. I love to share meals with family, friends, clients, prospects, acquaintances, and even complete strangers, who often become friends. I'm a big proponent of the phone. I like hearing that voice on the other end. Hearing the nuances in tone and being able to answer questions organically makes a massive difference when communicating. I like to host and attend social events, where I can mingle with people I know well, as well as those I want to know better. Sharing stories, information, laughs, and good humor seems to work much better in person.

As I've grown my business, I've often talked and met with other advisors who wanted to grow theirs. I've been happy to share my philosophy and process, which I call structural alpha. I know that some people will wonder why I'm helping the competition. After all, if other advisors learn my secrets, won't they take my clients?

I don't view other advisors as competition. I see those who do it right as the foundation and future of an industry that I love and want to see grow. Besides, to do it the right way requires a major sacrifice and an energy level that is unmatched in most industries. For those who can do it, I take my hat off to you, and I am proud to be with you in this industry.

Over the course of my career, it became clear to me that, rather than continuing to meet one-on-one, I could help many more advisors by writing a book. A book with actionable tips on how to grow an elite wealth management business the right way would, I thought, prove helpful.

I know there are other wealth management books out there, but this one really is different. This is not a theoretical book written by a consultant. It's a practical book written by someone who was once a newcomer, starting with nothing, and who has grown a successful decades-long elite wealth management practice—and is still in the trenches, growing his business today.

I also want to make it clear that I am not writing this book to make money; in fact, any profits from book sales will be contributed to highly rated charities that help underprivileged children in the United States. I've seen firsthand what a difference these groups make in a child's life—I met my foster son through Place of Hope in Palm Beach Gardens, Florida, and couldn't imagine life without him—and I want to do everything I can to support their mission, as well as those of other entities that help children.

I love this industry. I jump out of bed early every morning because I can't wait to get to work. My clients are some of the smartest people I know. I have learned so much from them and have become a better person and businessman as a result. Being an advisor has also allowed me to live a lifestyle that I couldn't have imagined as a child and has provided me with the opportunity to give back to others.

Part of giving back to others is giving back to the industry. I want others to learn what I've found so valuable in growing my practice. I will show you

- what worked for me and what didn't;

- how I prospected for clients and still do;

- why I receive many referrals without ever asking for them;

- how I manage my clients' portfolios and expectations;

- how I built a team (and am still building it);

- how I hire, compensate, and reward team members;

- how I manage the business and track metrics; and

- what I think of the future of the industry, and what I am doing to position myself for it.

I have seen nearly every tip, process, and strategy outlined in this book work in a real-life practice. I've also seen what doesn't work, and I will be pointing out those pitfalls.

So here is the book I wish I had years ago. Let me know if you find it useful. And if you have tips and tricks that I've missed, I'd love to hear them. I certainly do not pretend to have all the answers. There are many teams in the country that have more impressive client lists, have better investment performance, and produce more revenue than I do. That is why I, too, have an unquenchable thirst to improve every aspect of my own business. We're all in this together.[1]

---

1   Any advice and strategies discussed herein may not be suitable for your situation and are not intended as a solicitation or personalized recommendation for investment advice, products, or services. You should consult with a professional where appropriate. The views expressed herein are those of the author and do not necessarily represent the views of the organization for which he is employed, nor its officers, directors, or other employees. Neither the author nor the publisher shall be liable for any loss of profit or any other commercial damages, including but not limited to special, incidental, consequential, or other damages.

CHAPTER 1

THE FAMILY BUSINESS IS NOT FOR ME

"SON, YOU BETTER STUDY, because you obviously can't go into the family business. You don't have a mechanically inclined bone in your body."

My grandfather Salvatore "Pop" Ferrara—my namesake—would look at me and just shake his head. He ran a construction firm that had been founded in the early 1900s, when his father came over from Italy. My cousin runs it today, but construction wasn't what I was born to do, though not from lack of trying. My grandfather used to pick me up at home or school and take me to job sites. He was baffled by my inability to drive a nail straight with a hammer.

"Why can't you hit a stationary nail with a hammer when you can hit a moving puck with a stick or a curveball with a bat?"

His gruffness used to bother me, but I soon figured out he was this way with everybody. It really wasn't personal. On the other hand, he was the first one to buy us new skates or a baseball glove if the family budget couldn't cover them that month.

I think Pop would be surprised to learn that my relationship with him has served me so well in my business career. I learned not to take things personally—no one can control how someone else acts, only how you react—which is crucial when dealing with clients. But more than that, he taught me to be aware of the needs of others. I consider my clients an extension of my family and never lose sight of the fact that if it were not for them, I wouldn't have a business.

Pop also gave me one of the greatest pieces of advice I've ever received. I can still hear his voice in my head saying, "You have to have alligator skin to succeed in this world." That was the mentality of the European immigrants who came to the United States for a better life and often found themselves less than welcomed. But they persevered, and most were able to eventually provide a good living for their family—though it sometimes took a generation or two.

Having alligator skin—not letting things bother me and throw me off my game—became my mentality. It served me well when playing sports, and it has proved to be exactly what I needed as I grew my business.

My parents also had a massive impact on how I view the world, and how I treat my clients.

My father is my best friend. I speak with him every day. He's also one of my great role models. Through his actions—whether as the best coach I've ever had or as a responsible family man—he taught me that great leaders lead by example. They inspire loyalty and motivate others because they practice what they preach. They don't ask more of others than they ask of themselves.

My dad was one of the hardest workers I've ever known. He spent thirty-five years as a postal worker. When he retired, he had over eighteen months of sick leave built up. He simply told the post office to "give it to someone who needs it."

After he retired from the post office, he worked with me for ten years at Bear Stearns, answering phones and communicating with clients. He knew how to connect with clients and make each one feel like a close friend and the most important person in the world.

There were times when clients would return my call and get carried away talking to my father about their grandchildren or the Red Sox-Yankees rivalry or a recent event in the news. They would forget why they called me and hang up. I would look at him and say, "Dad, where did my biggest client go?"

While my dad gave me a work ethic to be proud of and a model of how to lead, my mother taught me to believe in myself. She taught me to fight for what is right and be generous to everyone. She loves to entertain and showed me how to make the effort to build strong bonds. I still receive a text every Sunday morning from my mother asking when I'll be coming over for pasta. I can come alone, with my entire family, or tell her I'm bringing twenty friends. She will always have enough food and always welcome company.

THE RIGHT BUSINESS FOR ME

Pop was right about me not being a good fit for the family business. I was never going to be able to drive a nail straight or remodel a kitchen. That meant I needed to find something else.

I am a first-generation college graduate, and I was very fortunate to get recruited to play hockey at Dartmouth College. A college hockey teammate, who was three years older, landed a job at Kidder Peabody after his graduation. He called me several times during his first year at the firm to tell me he thought that I was cut out for the business and that I needed to take a serious look at it. I was just a sophomore in college at the time, but I was anxious to get a head start on a career choice. I subscribed to the *Wall Street Journal*, majored in economics, and read as many books on the industry as I could. After reading the first book—I think it was *How to Earn $100,000 in Your First Three Years as a Stockbroker*—I was hooked. I was also fortunate enough to get an internship after my junior year at a financial services firm, which cemented my view that my former teammate was right. Financial advising was exactly what I was cut out for.

In *Outliers: The Story of Success,* Malcolm Gladwell looks at some of the highest-profile innovators of our time, people like Larry Ellison and Bill Gates, and explains how they were able to do what they did. One of his theories is that they came into their businesses with the right experience at the right time. They were smart, they made good use of opportunities, they worked really diligently—but they had the added advantage of being in the right place at the right time. I don't have anywhere near the talent of those people, but I definitely benefited from advantageous times.

I like to think that I entered the financial advisory business during its golden period. Individual retirement plans, private investment funds, tax-advantaged vehicles, personalized financial plans, and other strategies were just beginning to take hold and become available to the everyday private investor. Doctors, lawyers, entrepreneurs, and corporate executives could now use the strategies long used by family offices and institutional investors to generate stable, long-term returns and income. The need for financial advisors to help guide these well-off investors through the variety of new products and strategies was growing exponentially as people realized using an advisor wasn't just for the ultra-wealthy; it was for everyone who wanted to grow their assets and retire one day.

I was lucky enough to be born just after the baby boomer generation. In my opinion, this generation likes to do business with someone who is old enough to be experienced, yet young enough to help them pass their wealth on to the next generation. That describes those of us born between the baby boomers and the millennials.

Baby boomers control at least 70 percent of all disposable income in the United States and will be passing down about $30 trillion to the next generation.[2] Advising them on their retirement and estate needs is the perfect place to be right now. Being the right age, having the right experience and living in the right place have made being able to grow my business easier than at other times in history, but it still takes lots of work. I'd say it takes a lot more than the ten thousand hours of practice that Gladwell postulates are needed to become an expert. And in reality, though I like to think I was born at the perfect time, *any time* is the perfect time to get into this business if you have the right mindset and work ethic.

At the time I entered the business, financial services companies and banks were still willing to invest in training new advisors. Specific one- to two-year training programs let us rotate through various types of advising and banking functions to find the niche that best fit our talents and personalities. The goal was for us to be trained at headquarters and then branch out to various offices to train others.

When I graduated college, I was fortunate enough to be accepted into Drexel Burnham's eighteen-month intensive sales training program (IST). We met every workday at seven o'clock in the morning to listen to the firm's research call. The training involved three-month rotations through the various sales and trading desks, as well as a rotation where we worked under a research analyst. We also spent a two-month period of eight hours per day in a classroom, where we had professors from the New York Institute of Finance hone our finance skills. The last rotation was in the brokerage office marketing (mostly cold-calling back then) for an established advisor. On the first day of this assignment, I got to the office a half hour early and waited for the manager to arrive. When he came in, I introduced myself as one of the trainees who was there to help prospect for the advisors in the office. I told him I was going to work my tail

---

off and asked him if he could do me a favor—place me with the best new-account opener in the office. It was a bit aggressive of me to do, but the manager respected me for asking and granted me my wish. It was during this period of cold-calling that I knew I would make it.

I worked diligently, just as I had said I would. I took notes while this advisor put into practice the techniques we had learned in our training classes. He was a real pro on the phone. But as I watched and learned, I also realized that I was not in awe of anything he said, and, in fact, I was less in awe of his work ethic—he didn't actually have much of a drive. I showed up every morning at seven to listen to the morning research call, and often I would wait until after nine for this advisor to show up for work. If he opened a new account in the morning (which I had teed up for him), he would take a break to chat with the other brokers in the "bull pen." He would leave for lunch every day and was gone for the night by four thirty. If he could be the best in the office with this work schedule, I knew I could be, too. I knew nobody would outwork me, and I knew I would care about my clients more than he did. I couldn't wait to get started on my own.

During this period, the training class met every Tuesday night. Each trainee had to write a sales script and pitch it to our team leader in front of our entire class of twenty. Our team leader was very tough but fair. He would often rip apart trainees right in the middle of their pitch. Some of my fellow trainees would get rattled by this, but I relished it. The more intense it got, the better I felt I did. Having alligator skin certainly came in handy during these sessions.

During these training days, we not only learned the industry, but we learned what it meant to be professional. We learned how to promote ourselves and our company, all while putting the client first. And we learned what it took to grow our own business. I didn't realize it at the time (probably because I was only getting paid $20,000 my first year out of college living in New York City with student loans to pay off), but this training would be crucial to my future success, as well as to that of other advisors coming into the business at that time. It was also crucial to maintaining the industry's high standards and professionalism. I don't think there was ever a training program better than that one!

Because of the margin squeeze in the industry and subsequent bear markets, most financial services companies and banks had eliminated this specialized training by the early 2000s. They were struggling with massive losses (some actually went out of business), and it was just too expensive. I think that decision was shortsighted, but I can understand where it was coming from. Today, there are very few formal training programs left. Many firms will hire kids out of college or grad school to work on a team. The new hire will be asked to perform a specific role on that team, without really understanding how to truly give proactive advice and service the affluent or ultra-high-net-worth clients.

It has always been challenging to grow a successful financial advisory business, even with the best training in the industry. But life got exponentially more difficult after the 2008 financial crisis, as many investors began to actively turn against the industry. Many were angry that their advisor had not protected them better during the downturn. Others doubted that the advisors were really working in the clients' best interests, and instead were simply pushing their own overpriced products and churning accounts for profit. (Frankly, there are too many advisors in the business who were and are still doing just that.) Add in some high-profile financial scandals, such as Bernie Madoff's Ponzi scheme or a couple of the consumer banks' profit-generating ploys, and many current and prospective clients have a less-than-stellar view of the industry. They just don't trust that advisors are truly on their side.

This isn't just my opinion. It's borne out in survey after survey. For example, a 2016 poll by the American Association of Individual Investors (AAII) found that 65 percent of respondents said they mistrust the financial services industry to some degree; only 2 percent of respondents claimed to trust financial professionals "a lot," while 15 percent say they trust them "a little."[3] This distrust has pushed many to oversee their own financial investments and planning.

After reading a few books on investment and financial planning, or seeing articles on the internet, or watching infomercials late at night, the cohort that would normally be turning to advisors to plan their retirement can now often be found using online do-it-yourself programs or robo advisors. They use exchange-traded funds, index funds, target date funds, automatic rebalancing formulas, and other passive investment strategies. Many believe they can't do any worse than the high-priced professionals who didn't see the financial crisis coming.

If the industry is to right itself and prosper, we need to raise our standards and embrace best practices that promote trust by putting the client first. I consider it my duty to be on call for my clients at all times and go above and beyond what the normal advisor would do. My clients are wealthy families that have chosen me from any number of advisors available to them. As such, they expect me to educate myself and stay current with the best techniques and technology. They expect my team to be composed of the best and brightest people I can find. And they expect me to work at a firm that can be a one-stop shop for their needs. In other words, I surround my clients

---

3   Backman, "Most Americans Don't Trust Their Financial Advisors. Should They?"

with *structural alpha,* which puts me in a position to provide answers to their questions and be indispensable to their futures.

And that's where this book comes in. Without the training programs common twenty years ago, it is difficult for the industry to promote best practices, and it is even harder for advisors to learn them. People new to the field end up on their own, reinventing the wheel as they progress in their careers. I wrote this book to provide you with a system I've found tremendously helpful in acquiring and maintaining wealthy clients, and thus growing my business. It's a system built on specific activities and processes that connect me with my clients and their families and generate the trust needed to provide the type of high-level service affluent clients (actually any clients) need.

This system has a basis in programmable tactics and strategies, but it takes a specific set of soft skills to implement those actions. The following chapter outlines several keys to success and explains how embracing these soft personality skills will provide the foundation for growing your practice.

CHAPTER 2
TOP 10 KEYS FOR SUCCESS

I STARTED OFF WITH NOTHING. That might be the best place for anyone to start because you have nothing to lose. You can take chances and find what works best given your goals, temperament, and skills. Through trial and error, I've grown my business to the point where my clients entrust me with several billion dollars. These clients are all families or individuals, not institutions. I like to do business with real people instead of corporate entities, because it is easier to develop personal relationships. To me, this business is all about relationships and becoming indispensable to your clients, which I call *structural alpha*. As noted right at the front of this book, structural alpha is the value we create in our clients' lives from our advice on better

KEYS FOR SUCCESS

1. Educate yourself.

2. Think like an entrepreneur.

3. It's all about people.

4. This business is difficult; don't give up.

5. Have a game plan; be systematic.

6. Play to your strengths.

7. Be professional/trustworthy.

8. You can't do it all alone.

9. Practice what you preach.

10. Be humble.

TO ME, THIS BUSINESS IS ALL ABOUT RELATIONSHIPS AND BECOMING INDISPENSABLE TO YOUR CLIENTS, WHICH I CALL STRUCTURAL ALPHA ways to structure, organize, and plan for their family needs and goals. It is a systematic, methodical approach that enables you and your team to be indispensable in the eyes of your clients.

In the early years, I had the benefit of a formal training program that got me started on the right path, but no training program can cover everything. And it's the things that aren't covered that can make the difference between a business that is simply OK and one that is sought out by wealthy families and individuals to become their lead long-term (and, hopefully, lifelong) advisor.

Over time, I've identified a set of principles or actions that have been, and continue to be, instrumental to my success. As long as I've followed these keys to success, my business has thrived. Whenever I've drifted a bit, my business has suffered. I'll be digging into these keys in greater detail in later chapters and providing concrete steps you can take to implement them, but the following is an overview of what is to come.

KEY 1: EDUCATE YOURSELF

Never stop learning. Advisors succeed by knowing everything there is to know about their industry niche, their clients' business sectors, their community, and even their competition. Successful advisors immerse themselves in the financial services business and in the business of their target market. They are able to talk intelligently about the subjects that interest their clients as well as provide expert financial advice. The world is full of information, and the internet has made it easier than ever to access. Elite advisors devour the obvious research reports from all over Wall Street and business publications such as the *Wall Street Journal* and *Barron's,* but they also follow local news, world news, politics, and sports, and they keep up on best-selling fiction and nonfiction, trending movies and cultural topics. In other words, it is a never-ending process to be current.

Elite advisors also throw themselves into the process of learning everything they can about the various aspects of wealth management. I could always read a balance sheet and income statement, and I had a knack for picking stocks, but early in my career, I wasn't well-versed in estate planning, lending, or banking. I knew I needed those skills, so I started reading everything I could get my hands on. I still read everything I can get my hands on. Advisors looking to stay current in the industry can also educate themselves by obtaining their CFP, CFA, CIMA, CPWA, and other designations and licenses. They can go to conferences. They can strike up conversations in their day-to-day lives. The options for continuing to learn are limited only by time and imagination.

There is a lot to know, so commit yourself to being a lifelong learner.

KEY 2: THINK LIKE AN ENTREPRENEUR (BECAUSE YOU ARE ONE!)

Being a successful investment advisor isn't just about making good investment decisions. It's about being a successful entrepreneur and making good business decisions. This means you need to have the same mindset as any other entrepreneur. Entrepreneurs invest in their businesses. They invest in their communities. They aren't frivolous with their money—the dot.com days of marble fountains in the lobby are long over—but they aren't cheap. They know they need to spend money to make money.

I spend several hundred thousand dollars per year on growing my business. For an advisor to put this much capital into the business often means cutting back elsewhere. It might mean living somewhat frugally until the advisor is well established. For example, someone who is focused on growing a practice would forego buying a big home or expensive car with that first big check, and would instead plow that income back into the company. This is exactly what I did early in my career. Instead of purchasing a new car, I hired an assistant.

And even once established, living below one's means in order to invest more in the business pays massive dividends in the end. Delayed gratification works if you block and tackle well every day. Thinking like an entrepreneur also means always moving forward—always finding new ways to obtain clients, attract top level talent, and understand the bottom line. Advisors who are independent and own their company probably already understand this. But even those who work for a larger bank or brokerage firm will find it advantageous to understand margins and bottom lines so they can communicate effectively with their firm when they need more resources.

KEY 3: IT'S ALL ABOUT PEOPLE

All too often, financial advisors focus on performance and think that is all that matters. It's true that affluent clients want a reasonable return on their investments, but that's a given, like having a roof on your house. A buyer doesn't pay extra for a roof—the extra is for a prime location or added amenities. Advisors who set themselves apart offer much more than simply decent returns. They position themselves as people clients can turn to for help in every part of their lives.

This industry is not only about running computer algorithms and developing objective investment plans. It's about connecting with clients and doing what is best for each individual. Advisors who practice structural alpha find that their clients will ask their opinion on a variety of subjects, most of which have nothing to do with finances. These advisors are the center of a client's advisory universe, whether it involves finances, finding a restaurant able to handle a party of twenty, or locating the best doctor in the region. These successful advisors know that they won't be able to answer every question—and that's OK. What sets these advisors apart, however, is their willingness to exhaust all possibilities to find the answer, and to respond to the client as quickly as possible. That's how they make themselves indispensable.

Any advisor should be able to put together an investment strategy that meets the client's needs. But the financial advisor who rises to the top is the one who also becomes the client's family advisor. That's the reason some advisors become the advisor to the wealthy and others don't.

KEY 4: THIS BUSINESS IS DIFFICULT; DON'T GIVE UP!

Someone once told me that the financial advising industry was extremely competitive and that being a great advisor was "more difficult than being a middle linebacker in the NFL." Fortunately for me, I was born with the gift of gab, my body doesn't require much sleep, I have a tremendous amount of energy, and I care about people. I'm also competitive—and I have alligator skin.

But even with a winning personality, it's not easy. This business really is more perspiration than inspiration. What's important to remember is that everyone hits roadblocks and sometimes comes to a complete standstill. The trick is to stay professionally persistent. Always be prepared when meeting prospects. Look for ways to stay motivated. Be thick skinned. Successful advisors expect growing a business to be difficult, so challenges don't surprise them and throw them off their game. They know that's just the nature of the business and they keep going.

The sports world is full of stories of players who weren't the best athlete on the team but who overcame their limits through hours of work. No one can say that Tom Brady of the New England Patriots just relies on his talent. He was lightly regarded when coming out of college, and he was not drafted until the sixth round. No one would have pegged him as a future superstar. But he has a famously impressive work ethic plus the drive to learn everything he can about the game. His work ethic has served him well, helping him overcome doubters in the beginning of his career, a knee injury in the middle of it, and claims that he is "too old" most recently.

Hustle, effort, and work are things you can embrace, whether you are naturally talented or not. The financial advising business is just as difficult—or maybe even more difficult—than succeeding in a professional sport. But it can be conquered by those willing to consistently put in the work and not be discouraged when things aren't going smoothly. Setbacks are temporary if you stay in the game. As Wayne Gretzky famously once said, "You miss 100 percent of the shots you don't take."

I had a major setback in 2008 that could have driven me from the industry if I had let it. It was a perfect storm: Anything that could go wrong, did. The market was plummeting, resulting in all of our portfolios losing significant value. My employer was on the verge of default, and many of my clients moved their accounts to other investment firms. Some of my largest clients were executives of a major telecommunications company that got clobbered in the bear market, resulting in several having to withdraw a lot of capital from their accounts. Before I knew it, I had lost nearly 50 percent of my assets under management. I know every advisor who was in the business at that point will always remember those days. Many advisors left the business; I could have, too. Instead, I clung to the knowledge that this business will always have ups and downs. I just needed to put my head down and work through it. I revamped my business model, looked for opportunities in the new investment environment, and didn't give up. And because I didn't give up, almost all of my clients stayed with me. Those who left came back. It can't be said too often—this is a people business, and it was people who helped me recover.

KEY 5: HAVE A GAME PLAN

A game plan gives you a strategy and enables you to track your progress. Entrepreneurs—and those who run their own businesses are, by definition, entrepreneurs—need to know how well they are doing. Guessing won't do it. Feeling like they are making progress won't do it. They need to be able to look at numbers and see if they are reaching their goals. If they are, then they carry on. If they're not, seeing where they're falling short allows them to adjust their strategies and game plan before they go too far down the wrong road.

Sound game plans also provide strategies for when things go wrong, so adjustments can be made quickly without panicking. Making decisions when under pressure often makes a bad situation worse. A game plan made during calm periods provides a path that helps a business get through the rough times. How often have you seen a team that is losing at halftime come out of the locker room and completely turn things around? They didn't become better players during that twenty-minute break. But they did come up with a better game plan. They were able to adjust because the coaches had undoubtedly drawn up several plans that could be refined and implemented if the original plan wasn't working. Having these Plan Bs on hand makes it much more likely that good decisions will be made when the stakes are high.

To be effective, game plans need to be executed consistently and with laser focus. A systematic process—i.e., a methodical, repeatable approach—helps keep things from falling through the cracks. It also helps a business work through the down times. If an advisor continues to repeat the rainmaking or customer service steps, eventually revenues will begin flowing again. Systems are crucial to tracking progress, turning acquaintances into prospects, and prospects into clients.

KEY 6: PLAY TO YOUR STRENGTHS

Advisors with thriving, elite practices have learned to play to their strengths while mitigating their weaknesses. Each advisor is different, but a few qualities stand out in those who reach the top:

- Organization—As a practice grows, time-management skills will become crucial.

- Economic soundness—Having a financial cushion enables a practice to survive the ups and downs of the market.

- Focus—The industry has several niches. Advisors typically choose one or two, such as the business development side or the investment side, to focus on.

- Leadership—An advisor with a growing practice will need to gather and lead a great team in order to work with affluent clients.

It is often difficult to realistically assess yourself. Sometimes we don't recognize our strengths, or we downplay our weaknesses. This is a time when an outside coach can come in handy. If you don't have a coach or mentor, you can ask a colleague or even your partner. (But also begin looking for that mentor!) A lot of the characteristics needed to build a successful wealth management business are the same as those needed to sustain a long-term friendship. Anyone who knows you, and whose judgment you trust, can act as a sounding board to help you pinpoint what you do really well and what you need to work on.

Once you know your strengths as an advisor, you can work to focus on those strengths while improving your weaknesses. We all love to focus on our strengths. Those are the things about ourselves that we like best. You want to play to your strengths, but at the same time you can't let your weaknesses drag you down. In fact, working on our weaknesses, either by improving on them directly or by hiring people who are strong in those areas, can have a much greater impact on our business.

The important thing is to take the time to really know yourself. Then you can offer your best to your clients.

KEY 7: BE PROFESSIONAL/TRUSTWORTHY

TRUSTWORTHINESS

Pop Ferrara once told me right before he retired that in his sixty years in the construction business, he never signed a written contract. He told me that he never needed a written contract because his word was his bond. If he looked a customer in the eye and shook hands, he honored his price and deadlines to get the work done. Because he honored his word and did great quality work, he had a lot of repeat customers and many unsolicited referrals. Obviously, we are in a different day and age, and nobody would perform work without a written contract that spelled out the terms of the expected work. However, the lesson behind the story still holds true—keep your word and make it your bond.

The foundation of this, and any, business is clients. And the glue that keeps advisors and clients together is trustworthiness. Getting your first clients isn't as challenging as keeping them over the long term. How advisors treat their clients is a key determinant when it comes to predicting their success.

Clients want to trust their advisor to safeguard and grow their wealth. They are trusting an outsider with the security of their families. Nothing kills a business faster than a reputation for playing fast and loose with clients' money. Once you've sullied your reputation, it's almost impossible to recover.

You've seen this before: Michael Jackson. Martha Stewart. O.J. Simpson.

The financial services business certainly has its own infamous falls from grace. Bernie Madoff and Allen Stanford will forever be known for their Ponzi schemes rather than their business acumen. Frankly, there have been so many examples of fraud that many wealthy individuals are understandably wary of our industry. But I look at that as an opportunity. If my clients know my word is my bond and trust me, they will stay with me and refer their friends to me.

PROFESSIONALISM

I can't emphasize enough that this industry needs to raise its standards around professionalism. People who are reading this book, the ones who want to do things the right way, can be part of that change. Typically, when an investment information sheet is arranged, the data on the security or investment is on the left side. This is because this is the first thing investors want to know about. Then, moving from left to right, there's a column for terms, and then a column for the commission or fee at the far end. Too many advisors in the industry read from right to left. They look at their commission or fee first, then determine whether the security is a good fit for their clients. There is no room in this business for such behavior.

I have always believed that if I did the right thing for my client first, I would be more than compensated for it in the long run. Early on in my career, I recall the traders on the over-the-counter (OTC) desk taking down blocks of stock that were purchased between the bid and ask prices. For instance, if the stock traded at a bid of $6.00/share and was being offered at $6.50/share, the desk from time to time might have been able to purchase a block of stock at $6.25/share. They then would advertise to the sales force they had a "special": the advisors could offer it to their clients at $6.50/share and mark it up at least $0.25/share so the client would see the confirmation of the trade at $6.75 per share and think he was being charged $0.25/share (which is 3.7 percent), when in fact the true commission was $0.50/share (end price to client of $6.75/share minus the true cost of $6.25/share that the desk purchased it at) or 7.4 percent! Thankfully, these "specials" have disappeared in the industry.

More recently, in May 2018, regulations were changed to require all fixed-income trades to reflect the true cost on all confirmations. Many people in the industry were upset about this rule, but

I supported the change. I was on a conference call with several top advisors who were complaining about it. I jumped into the conversation and stated that I believed my own business would grow as a result. I have always been transparent with my clients and made sure they knew what their fee/commission was up front before anything was purchased. I felt that when some of my clients, who had relationships with other advisors, saw how much they were really being charged by these other advisors, they would move more assets to me, which is exactly what happened. Don't get me wrong, I don't work for nothing. I work for what I think is fair. But more importantly, I don't hide anything from my clients.

Professionalism is a bit nuanced, but you know it when you see it. Professionalism comes across in how you present yourself and in how you treat your clients. Your professionalism will show up in your office environment—in how your phone is answered, how quickly you or someone on your staff responds to clients, and your accessibility. You are dealing with a lot of money. Clients want to know they are dealing with a truly responsible advisor.

Being professional isn't a requirement imposed from the outside or a coat worn only at certain times. It needs to be part of who you are at your core. That means practicing what you preach. Lead by example—i.e., your own finances need to reflect your skill. Always make the ethical decision. In short, treat clients the way you'd treat family.

KEY 8: YOU CAN'T DO IT ALL ALONE

Today, it is very difficult to be a lone wolf and manage a successful practice yourself. The affluent want an advisor who can do it all. They want someone who can solve problems, who can help manage all of their financial needs. This takes a team, whether it is in-house or virtual. So today, I suggest a newcomer work on a successful team either for a major bank or an independent, where it will be possible, eventually, to take on more responsibility or even receive some equity. A successful team is one that has at least $500 million in assets, has a good work ethic, and has a deep desire to continue to grow its business and serve its clients. Once an advisor has developed some skills and a client base, a decision needs to be made as to whether to stay and build a practice as part of a larger team, or head out and form a new group.

Advisors who want their own practice need to put together a team they can trust. Every member of the team, however, doesn't need to be in-house. My in-house team is composed of members who provide deeper and broader support for my investment niche. Overlaid with my in-house group are outside professionals who provide additional skills in accounting, insurance, estate planning, small business succession, and other aspects of total wealth management. Building a team is so important that I've devoted a full chapter to it later in the book.

I also use outside coaches and mentors to help me focus and fine-tune my management and business skills. I just have to look back at my career to see what a difference a good coach can make. Every single jump in my business has occurred after I have connected with a coach. I have used many in my career, but the one who has had the most impact and on whom I still count today is Matt Oechsli of the Oechsli Institute. Over the past several years, the Oechsli Institute has helped me structure my team like a firm. Matt is still a trusted coach I bounce ideas off regularly. But just as when you are looking for the right partner in your personal life, you need to make sure the coach is a good fit. I've met some really good people who have some great ideas on how to improve my business—but they didn't connect with me. There's no shame in moving on to someone who does. It's no reflection on you or the coach. It's just the way things are. The coaches and mentors you connect with need to meet *your* needs, not someone else's. Also, do not hesitate to ask a more experienced and successful advisor for advice or an opinion. Asking someone for a favor or for help and then showing appreciation is actually flattering to that person. Most successful people are not only happy to help but want to help.

So don't be embarrassed to ask. The good guys in this industry want to pay it forward and make sure newcomers—or anyone who simply wants to take the next step—succeed. We can all benefit from someone who looks at our businesses with an objective eye and helps us grow. I'm still using coaches to help me move to the next level. I suspect I always will.

KEY 9: PRACTICE WHAT YOU PREACH

Clients won't trust you if they don't believe you practice what you preach. This is not a "do as I say, not as I do" business. I once had a prospect who was interviewing several advisors and wanted to know what he should be asking each one. I told him that from my viewpoint, he should be asking the advisors to explain how they managed their own personal portfolios and to supply three to five references. People in this business are often poor at managing their own money, because they are either too aggressive or overly conservative. I picked up my quarterly personal report dating back to 1994 and handed it to him, saying, "These are my own personal returns. I'm proud of the way I manage my own money, and if I can't manage money for myself, how can you expect me to make money for you or anyone else? Ask the other advisors for their personal portfolios—I bet they won't show them to you."

He came back to me a week later and said, "Not only did you win a portion of the business, but you won all of it. Nobody else even wanted to talk to me about their own personal portfolios."

Being able to prove that you take your own advice is one of the best ways of proving to a client that you can be trusted with their money.

KEY 10: STAY HUMBLE

Never forget you are in a service business. You are here to help your clients reach their goals, whether they be for a comfortable retirement or wealth for future generations. Be grateful for the chance to help. It's a role not many people get to have.

KEY TAKEAWAYS

- A successful wealth management business is based on relationship management—structural alpha.

- A successful wealth management business has a strong internal team and reciprocal relationships with other professionals.

- To succeed in wealth management, you must have alligator skin.

CHAPTER 3

RAINMAKING—BUILDING A PIPELINE

SIMPLY PUT, BEING A RAINMAKER revolves around bringing in new business. That means every successful business needs a rainmaker, and if it is your business, that rainmaker is probably you.

This is where many advisors falter. *To be a million-dollar producer, you must have $125 million in AUM generating an average of eighty basis points in fees—assuming you are 100 percent fee-based. To get to that point, you must build a pipeline of qualified prospects that is twice the size of your client base.* That means if you need one hundred clients to reach the $125 million level, you will need two hundred prospects in your pipeline. Now, numbers can vary. An advisor who focuses on households with a net worth of $50 million or above will need fewer clients. An advisor focused on the affluent, but not necessarily ultra-high net worth, will need more. But the bottom line is the same—an advisor is going to need an active and strong pipeline to get to where they want to be.

Reaching this number can seem overwhelming when you are starting from scratch. Making the number of calls and contacts to prospects needed to reach this level, or asking friends and acquaintances for their business, doesn't come easily to most people. Prospecting methods, however, don't have to be onerous. I've found several techniques that make reaching the one hundred-plus prospects goal very doable, as well as enjoyable. In fact, rainmaking can be the best part of the day if done right. No matter where you are in your career, you need an active pipeline of prospects to convert into clients if you want your business to grow. So you might as well embrace rainmaking!

Reframing what is being offered can make prospecting easier. Elite advisors are not selling a product. Every single one of their prospects can go on the internet, do their own research, and manage their own portfolio by investing in ETFs and mutual funds. The advisor's job is not to sell them a product or a service. Our job is to sit alongside our clients and help them gather and use the overwhelming amount of information out there appropriately, guide them through the minefield, protect them from stepping on the land mines, be a steward of their wealth, and educate them and their children along the way.

It is very similar to what a VIP or concierge doctor does. My concierge doctor oversees all of my medical needs. He has access to all of my medical records and coordinates appointments with specialists, if the need arises. Many times, the best specialists are not taking on more patients but will take a referral from my doctor. He also gives me an extensive physical once a year. He has a tremendous, attentive staff that answers phone calls and responds quickly and efficiently. I have access to his cell phone, and he is on call for his patients at any time. I remember a few summers ago, I was with my son at a baseball tournament out of state. It was a crucial summer for him because he was trying to earn a college baseball scholarship. This was the biggest tournament of the summer, and all the college scouts attended. The first night in the hotel room, he developed an infection that knocked him off his feet. I texted my concierge doctor at nine on a Saturday morning. Within a half hour, we were picking up antibiotics at a local pharmacy. Now that is service! My son was better in two days and didn't miss a day of baseball. By the end of the tournament, he had five Division 1 offers.

I am happy to pay a fee for a great doctor with a friendly and professional staff who goes out of his way for his patients. He has never asked me for a referral, but I have given him many. Who wouldn't want help from someone like that? This doctor now has a full practice, which he built almost exclusively through referrals, including mine.

This is the type of energy you want to build around your investment practice. Referrals are the pot of gold at the end of the rainbow and outstanding service is the primary driver of referrals.

BUILDING THE FOUNDATION FOR YOUR RAINMAKING PROCESS

Rainmaking is a very precise, thoughtful process. Before developing a targeted list or getting in front of that high-net-worth prospect, advisors need to have the right processes in place, as well as the right attitude, to sustain them through all the ups and downs of the business.

FIRST THINGS FIRST

- Before beginning a rainmaking campaign, every advisor should be familiar with a good customer relationship management (CRM) program. This will be invaluable as you launch a systematic campaign to grow a pipeline and convert prospects into clients.

- Services and business models should be easily articulated. What value proposition is being offered? What mission statement underlies the practice? A mission statement should be simple and concise, and everyone on the team should understand it. This is our mission statement: "Our team protects, manages, and transitions wealth for a limited number of families across the country."

- Elite advisors position themselves as solution providers, not as sales people. They develop relationships before they pitch their services.

- It's often said that some people are just born to be rainmakers. Don't believe it. Sure, rainmaking comes more naturally to some, but rainmakers are made, not born.

BE PREPARED

I am not going to get business from every prospect. Sometimes the fit or the timing just isn't right. But I'm never going to be eliminated because I wasn't prepared. In addition, whenever possible, I'm going to make the extra effort that sets me apart. For example, a few years ago I was competing for a new client. Prior to the first meeting, we had a "get to know you" phone call, where we talked about the client's investment objectives, as well as life in general. During this call, I learned that the family was planning a trip to China. Based on this call, I prepared for the first meeting, and I felt it went well. Before leaving, I pulled out a book on travel in China that I had purchased and gave it to the wife. A week later, I found out that I won the relationship. Obviously, the meeting went well, but the wife told me that she appreciated my thoughtfulness more than anything else. I didn't win the business because I promised better performance—no one can guarantee that. Instead, I won it by remembering it is the little things—particularly listening and being prepared—that encourage people to give you a shot and that set you apart.

When it comes to prospecting, my whole mindset is, "I'm getting the business." That doesn't mean that everything is always going to go my way—I've certainly had my share of setbacks—but I'm never going to fail due to lack of effort or preparation. I have found that almost without exception, when I put in the effort and take the time to prepare, the ratio of wins to losses increases significantly.

I tell my kids it's okay to fail, but don't fail because you didn't study. Don't fail because you didn't put in the time. I tell my son, "You want to be a great baseball player? You had better be in the batting cage every day. There are no shortcuts."

This business is 95 percent hard work and 5 percent glamour. It's doing the little things. It's blocking and tackling. I don't do things for the glamour. I do things because I want to be good at what I do, and I enjoy developing relationships with my clients.

BELIEVE YOU ARE GOING TO SUCCEED

It's important to develop a mindset of winning and learning not to fail. It's okay to miss your numbers on occasion or lose a client now and then, but no one should accept failure as the status quo. Getting new business is a numbers game, and advisors need to be thick-skinned. Every rainmaker is going to hear more "no" than "yes." Having something go wrong isn't failing. It's simply a roadblock. Failing is giving up. Dusting yourself off and carrying on is the road to success. Remember, this is a marathon, not a sprint. Have strategies ready to keep you going in the face of failure, and you'll rise to the top.

HAVE ALLIGATOR SKIN

A baseball player batting .300 has a great batting average, but that means he has failed to reach base safely 70 percent of the time. When I was prospecting during my early days, I failed to convert a prospect into a client about 90 percent of the time. Some people would hang up. Others would just say no before I could even get to my spiel. I had to have alligator skin. Today, I still prospect, but most of our clients come through referrals from clients or centers of influence. So, our closing rate has changed dramatically, to over 75 percent. However, I wouldn't have reached this point if I had let early rejection stop me.

STAY MOTIVATED

In life, motivation is the key to success. Some people are simply self-motivated and nothing seems to get them down. But most of us need to develop processes to keep us motivated when things aren't going well. In addition, we all need to find ways to stay motivated when things go really well. It's counterintuitive, but it's often easier to get motivated by challenges than to stay motivated when things are going smoothly and there is no challenge.

The fear of failure motivates me. Failing to meet industry or corporate goals doesn't motivate me as much as the fear of failing the high goals I've set for myself does. The fear of letting my clients down, my team down, my family down, and myself down pushes me to do the extras. Don't get me wrong, I fail at times—if I didn't, business and life would be boring. When I do fail, however, I never get depressed but simply focus more and persevere.

They say if you are feeling down, all you have to do is smile, and your whole mood will improve. Incorporating consistent processes in your prospecting will have much of the same effect when things aren't going well, and you are struggling to stay motivated. If you just keep doing what has proven successful in the past, your motivation will reemerge, and you'll be back to converting prospects into clients in no time.

Consistency in how you treat people is a critical leadership trait that very few people possess. If I can be consistent in my responses during volatile times, my clients, my team, and my family will be better off as a result. For me to stay consistent and be able to give my best, I need to live a balanced life. I need to have a healthy diet, exercise religiously, and get a regular amount of sleep (fortunately my body has never required a lot of sleep). I also know that showing up and putting the quality time in is vital to my success. I believe in karma, so I may regret admitting this, but in the thirty years I've been in the business, I have never taken a sick day. Remember when I said that my father had over eighteen months of sick days left over when he retired from the postal service? I like to think that a strong work ethic and commitment runs in the family.

CREATING A PROSPECT LIST

One of the largest challenges any advisor faces, whether new or experienced, is building and maintaining a prospect list. The standard suggestions on how to do this aren't bad—many, if not most, advisors succeed using standard practices—but I have found a few tweaks that make the standard suggestions more efficient.

CHALLENGE:

How do I create a prospect list?

STANDARD SUGGESTION:

Cast a wide net.

Send scattershot postcards and/or emails to everyone within certain zip codes. Place ads in upscale publications or through Google. If you get your name in front of enough people, you're sure to get some to talk to you.

BETTER SUGGESTION:

Cast a very narrow but deep net.

I attract more qualified prospects when I focus on specific market segments, geographies, or demographics. Where advisors focus will be based on where they work, and/or what they are good at, but there are some very specific steps that can be taken to narrow the focus.

1. UNDERSTAND THE MARKET

There are an almost infinite number of investment specialties—family office, corporate benefits, alternative investments, pension funds, insurance, fixed income, estate planning, wealth management, etc. Some of these specialties have more opportunities than others. Finding those opportunities is the key to success. Talk to other successful advisors. What trends do they see in the market? Talk to other professionals who deal with wealthy individuals. What do their clients say they wish their advisors offered? Advisors who work for larger firms can ask their managers what the most successful producers are doing to separate themselves from the pack.

2. DETERMINE THE TYPES OF CLIENTS YOU WANT TO ATTRACT

As advisors get deeper into their due diligence, they soon begin to zero in on the part of the industry that appeals to them and where they see the opportunities. These opportunities will revolve around clients, so once an advisor has honed in on a particular industry niche, it is time to narrow the focus further to specific types of clients. Some advisors are interested in young professionals. Others focus on entrepreneurs, inherited wealth, family offices, or retirees. Instead of a client type, some advisors look at specific industries. Maybe they want to be part of a sports management team and handle the finances of athletes. Or maybe they want to focus on the investment needs of entertainers or scientists or corporate executives. Your due diligence on the industry should lead you to define the type of clients you want to work with and what problems you can solve for them. That will form the foundation of your business. Areas of expertise typically change over time as industries and demographics change. The key is to never stop learning and always be on the lookout for rainmaking opportunities.

3. DEVELOP A GAME PLAN FOR CONNECTING WITH PROSPECTS

Once an advisor has focused on a specific industry niche and client demographic, the next task is to develop a focused, professional strategy or game plan to connect with prospects. This step is so important that we'll go over how to do this in detail later in the chapter.

4. BE PATIENT

Growing a business doesn't happen overnight. It almost always takes longer than anyone thinks. In most cases, it will take at least three to five years. But don't give up. If you are doing it right and you show consistency, you'll reach your goal in the end.

5. HAVE A PLAN B

No one should develop one game plan and assume that is sufficient. You always need to have a Plan B for when things change (they will) or you run into a roadblock (you will). I have had to reinvent myself more than once. And each time, I was able to come out on top because I developed a game plan in advance that allowed me to prepare and be ready for the challenges I faced.

CHALLENGE:

How do I connect with the prospects on my list?

STANDARD SUGGESTION:

Make lots of phone calls and send lots of mailings.

BETTER SUGGESTION:

*Develop a concentration and specialize in
an area so prospects want to talk with you.*

TO BE A SUCCESSFUL RAINMAKER, YOU HAVE TO GIVE PROSPECTS A REASON TO USE YOUR SERVICES RATHER THAN SOMEONE ELSE'S

To be a successful rainmaker, you have to give prospects a reason to use your services rather than someone else's. One way to do this is to become an expert for the specific clients you want to attract. For example, some advisors focus on working with doctors or medical professionals, others on executives of publicly traded companies, and others work with retirees only. Some set themselves up nicely with clients in a particular industry, such as technology or banking. Advisors can also develop a product niche. For instance, they can specialize in handling and managing corporate cash, corporate retirement plans, or alternative investments. The variations and niches are almost endless. The key is to know your specialty inside and out.

What you specialize in will depend on your interest and the opportunities around you. They usually develop over time. When you develop a concentration, rainmaking becomes very narrow and deep. Here are a few ways to approach becoming a specialist:

- Learn the investment needs of a specific niche by talking to practitioners in that arena.

- Talk to members of the target market to find out what they need.

- Take classes, get certifications and read books to learn any technical aspects unique to the investment needs of a specific market.

- Learn about the industry itself—subscribe to trade publications, attend conferences, network with industry executives. Prospects typically feel more comfortable talking to people who can talk their language.

I took these steps myself when I was starting my practice. Back in the mid to late nineties, discount brokerage firms were beginning to proliferate. It wasn't long before we saw the emergence of online trading. After learning as much as I could about the niches that composed the industry, I decided the best way to differentiate myself from the discount brokers was to become an expert at handling the restricted stock needs of corporate executives of publicly traded companies. To narrow the universe and be most efficient, I focused on industries that awarded the most stock options to executives at the time—technology, telecom, and healthcare.

Once I had settled on my target universe, I had to educate myself. I studied the ins and outs of restricted stock as well as the process of executing the cashless exercise of stock options and how to arrange a loan for my clients to execute it. I learned the differences, advantages, and disadvantages between non-qualified and incentive stock options (ISOS). I worked on the best ways to deal with the corporate counsel of a publicly traded company, how to set up 10b5-1 plans, and how to make sure they were correctly disclosed, as well as to mitigate taxes.

I was then able to begin building a prospect list in earnest. First of all, I immersed myself in the nitty-gritty details of the technology, telecom, and healthcare industries. It's easier to interact and carry on conversations with executives if you can talk intelligently about their industry trends and challenges.

I built a list of executives and inputted everything about them into my database. I built distribution lists, and every month I mailed (then eventually emailed) our firm's published research to the executives it pertained to.

My firm (Bear Stearns at the time) became an invaluable resource, as I was able to provide proprietary research reports to prospects, as well as to invite them to our conferences. I got to know the investment bankers and analysts at Bear Stearns who dealt with the executives in my targeted industries, and I made sure that they knew this was my area of focus.

It took a systematic approach and an abundance of staying power, but eventually the bankers and analysts considered me qualified enough to entrust their own clients to me. Referrals from my own firm became a steady source of prospects when growing my business and leveraged my time in obtaining clients.

Becoming very adept at handling the restricted stock needs of corporate executives was a means to an end. I wasn't looking at these trades to grow my business. Instead, I was looking at them to be a foot in the door and the beginning of long-term relationships. These clients had the majority of their net worth tied up in their own company's stock, so it was prudent for them to diversify their holdings. My goal was to convince them to use my team to put together an appropriate asset allocation that was prudent for them. I was very direct and transparent with these new clients. I told them up front that I was good at handling their restricted stock needs but believed I could be even more valuable to them and their families if they allowed me to protect, manage, and transition their wealth. I told them my goal was to work with them for many decades. Fortunately, many hired me, but before they would transfer significant portions of their wealth to me, I had to gain their trust with small steps.

Typically, I would start out by taking a portion of the cash we now had from selling the restricted stock options and invest it at the bottom of the risk matrix into tax-free municipal bonds or similar conservative investments. As my clients became more familiar with my investment philosophy, they would trust me with additional allocations and we would move up the risk spectrum into more growth-oriented investments. My job was not to make my clients wealthy—they had already become wealthy when they converted some of their restricted shares. Instead, my job was to help them develop a plan appropriate to their specific situation and goals, protect and preserve their newfound wealth, and give them a decent rate of return without undue risk. If something unexpected were to happen in the market, they didn't have to worry about the assets I was managing.

While I certainly look for a decent rate of return, I really aim to protect against the downside, because that downside can be devastating. For example, in 1999, there were 457 IPOs, many of which were internet- and technology-related. Of those 457 IPOs, 117 doubled in price on the first day of trading.[4] This is the type of performance that makes clients clamor to get in on the action. In fact, my firm

---

4   Beattie, "Market Crashes: The Dotcom Crash (2000-2002)."

was involved in some of these IPOs, and because our bankers and analysts considered me an expert, so was I. That means that it was possible for me to place clients in these stocks. But even in the face of pressure from clients, I urged caution. These were speculative stocks. There would be winners, but there would also be losers.

In 2001 the number of IPOs dwindled to seventy-six, and none of them doubled on the first day of trading. From March 11, 2000, to October 9, 2002, the Nasdaq Composite lost 78 percent of its value as it fell from 5046.86 to 1114.11![5] Fortunately, because of a proper asset allocation and attention to downside protection, many of my clients from those days are still with me today.

But, when it came to future prospecting, welcome to Plan B …

A few years after the Nasdaq market crash, my family and I relocated to Florida. At that point, the business had changed, and although I still handled many executives of publicly traded companies, the opportunities were not as great, as many stock options were now underwater. I came up with a new game plan and a new way to differentiate myself. As before, I needed to study the market and find a specialized niche that would set me apart from other advisors. So, I dove in and began analyzing the financial landscape around me.

Florida has a large population of retirees. Because there is no state income tax, Florida also has a lot of wealthy people who move here from higher-tax states. Put those two demographics together, and it was obvious that my best plan was to become an expert on retirement planning—financial planning, cash flow analysis, budgets, etc.—and tax planning.

To do that, my team and I immersed ourselves in the details of wealth management for retirees and executives who wanted to use tax-efficient strategies. I contacted the best tax attorneys in the area

5   Ibid.

to learn everything I could about those strategies. I dove in to understand how executive retirement plans work.

Then I went further. When I started out, I subscribed to all the medical and technical journals and publications that my target executives did. I went to their conferences. I needed to know what they were facing. I needed to be able to talk to them about what was happening in their professions. I needed to be one of them.

It's the same with retirees and those looking for tax-efficient strategies. I'm not at retirement age yet, but I can understand what they are looking at. And I moved from Massachusetts to Florida, just as many of my clients did, so I absolutely understand the desire to pay less in taxes.

If you *are* actually one of them, this gives you a real edge. In addition to my advisory practice, I own two other businesses. That means I can relate to the unique financial needs of entrepreneurs, because I face the same challenges. Other entrepreneurs know I understand them, so they trust me to handle their financial affairs, and I do a lot of business with this group.

I'm explaining what works for me not to blow my own horn, but to give you an idea of the effort, detail, and thought process that goes into differentiating yourself to gain an edge. Know and understand that most of your competition will not have the energy to do what it takes; your efforts will give you an advantage.

CHALLENGE:

How can I leverage others to provide me with prospects?

STANDARD SUGGESTION:

*Have family, friends, neighbors, anyone and everyone—
introduce you to people they know.*

BETTER SUGGESTION:

Ask for introductions to specific people.

Rainmakers are always on the lookout for new prospects. When I recognize that there is someone who might make a good prospect, I check all my contacts to see if I know anyone who might be acquainted with them. These contacts could include clients, friends, colleagues (who are not competitors, obviously), networking connections, and others in the community. You want to exhaust all possibilities for a connection to this prospect. Once you've identified a connection, ask for an introduction. Simply say, "I know Joe Smith belongs to your country club, and I think he might be a good fit with me. Can you introduce us?" This is not a referral or recommendation. The connection is only being asked to facilitate an introduction for a meet and greet. People are happy to help if you ask for a specific introduction. Asking, "Do you know someone who can use my services?" is much less effective because you are asking them to do the work of pinpointing prospects.

BETTER SUGGESTION:

Graciously accept and provide referrals.

As I mentioned previously, there is a difference between introductions and referrals. Introductions are simply putting you in contact with another person, while referrals are actually vouching for and recommending your business. I am very comfortable asking for an introduction, but I rarely, if ever, ask for referrals. Don't misunderstand me. Referrals are what every rainmaker looks for! But they are most powerful when they are spontaneously and freely given. Many people in this industry would disagree with this, and, in fact, do have success with asking for referrals. In my practice, however, waiting for referrals to come to me, rather than me chasing the referrals, has worked well.

According to the Oechsli Institute research, there is a major difference between asking for an introduction and asking for a referral. Eight out of every ten clients will be happy to introduce you to someone they know. That same number will feel awkward when you ask for a general referral—they feel imposed upon. However, they will be happy to refer you to friends if it occurs organically. The better you treat your clients, the more likely they are to provide unsolicited referrals. Oechsli Institute data also shows that the majority of advisors are not capitalizing on this phenomenon.[6]

When I was growing my business in Massachusetts, I ended up working with the top twelve executives of a Fortune 500 company based on a single referral from my parent firm. This company was an important client for the firm, and our bankers trusted me to handle one of the executive's stock options. Then, based on my performance

---

6   Oechsli, "4 Proven Financial Advisor Marketing Activities."

with this executive over time, I added some of the board members to my roster. At that point, other people were doing my prospecting for me. This is the Holy Grail for rainmakers—leveraging your time by having other centers of influence become advocates for you.

I've found several ways to increase unsolicited word-of-mouth referrals, so that now, nearly all of my new clients come to me because they know someone I already work with. Here are some of those ways:

- Those who are part of an investment bank have a built-in referral network. Bankers and other professionals in the firm can refer business to any number of internal advisors. Thus, we always make an effort to get to know these organizational professionals so that we are on their radar. We invite them to our events, where they get to know us personally, as well as to see what we do. Like anyone, they will refer more business to those they know and trust. Most importantly, when they refer clients to us, we make them look good by treating their clients well. We also repay the favor by referring clients back to them. Although I don't like to keep score with referrals, I do think it makes sense to favor centers of influence who provide referrals, as long as they provide superior service.

- Set up a network group of other professionals. Forming a network group isn't difficult, but it takes some time to identify the right members. An active networking group should have no more than ten people, but eight is an even better number because it is more manageable. Each member should be a professional working with wealthy individuals (or aspiring to work with wealthy individuals), and membership should be limited to one person per specialty. So, there might be one financial advisor, one CPA, one estate planning attorney and one general business attorney. There could also be a commercial and a residential high-end real estate realtor/broker, as well as a life and disability insurance expert, and a property and casualty insurance person. You can find these people by asking your current clients whether they are happy with their CPAs or attorneys. If they are, ask who they are and why they like them. You want to find other professionals who share your values of professional and customer service. You will probably end up with three or four names for each field. Carefully select the people you want to invite to the group. When extending an invitation, make sure everyone knows that this is a real commitment. If anyone misses more than two meetings of the twelve in the year, they are out of the group. That way, everyone takes it seriously. Select people who are of similar age and at the same level in their careers, well connected, and well educated. They should be visible in the community, involved in charitable endeavors, and on local boards. They also need to have a deep desire to grow their business. Don't keep score, but everyone in the group should be comfortable looking out for opportunities for each other and knowing that the others will make their clients look good if they give them a referral. The number of referrals will snowball, and everyone will grow together if you have the right people.

STANDARD SUGGESTION:

*Ask the people in your firm to give you
additional prospect lists to work with.*

BETTER SUGGESTION:

*Ask the best producers in your office
to let you work the bottom 20 percent of their books.*

Every top producer has a small percentage of clients and prospects who just aren't moving. Maybe the senior producer doesn't have time to work every prospect; maybe that producer just has favorite clients; maybe, for whatever reason, the advisor didn't hit it off with a few people. Maybe they are good clients, but they simply aren't large enough to grab the senior producer's full attention. These prospects aren't hot, but they aren't cold either.

Many established producers would be happy to consider working with a younger advisor to make sure the lower 10 or 20 percent of their prospects and clients are contacted on a regular basis. Because there is no template for this type of relationship, it would be up to the two advisors to negotiate what "work with" means. The producer might ask the younger advisor to connect with less-active prospects and clients, build relationships, and then let the producer know which of them have potential. The producer would then take over from there, giving the younger advisor a percentage of any commission or management fee realized. After the advisor is seen as competent, the producer might feel comfortable releasing the lower 10 percent, with the goal of increasing assets under management from current clients and transforming prospects into clients. It would be reasonable for the two "partners" to split the increased revenue fifty-fifty. If the advisor isn't able to develop these prospects, nothing is lost. But if the advisor does bring in additional revenue that the senior producer didn't have time to chase, it is a win-win situation.

The top producer wins by being able to continue to focus on the more active part of the book, while still realizing additional revenue from the less active portion, and the younger advisor is able to work a qualified list of households.

I did something similar to this in my younger days. A colleague introduced me to a senior producer, and I began prospecting for him. We became close friends, and we often had lunch together, during which he would tell me stories of how the industry had developed and how he worked with clients. Taking advantage of the knowledge and skills of those around you is good for you, good for your firm, and good for the industry.

When he retired, the firm arranged the sale of his book to me. This allowed him to monetize his book, while I received a cash-flowing asset and the opportunity to service those clients moving forward.

This scenario could become common in every major firm. The average age of today's advisor is sixty-two, which means that most of them are just a few years away from retiring. Those who work for a larger firm can easily find those senior advisors. Those who work for an independent company can find senior independents by contacting those who are clearing through the same custodial firm.

KEY TAKEAWAYS

- Successful rainmakers are specialists in their investment niches so that prospects want to talk to them.

- Successful rainmakers develop networking relationships with other centers of influence.

- The Holy Grail for rainmakers is a business based on referrals.

- Successful rainmakers are masters at the art of making the sale.

CHAPTER 4
RAINMAKING—CONVERTING PROSPECTS INTO CLIENTS

BUILDING A QUALIFIED PROSPECT list is just the beginning of the rainmaking process. The middle of the process is connecting with the prospects on the list, and the end is converting them into clients. If you are focused and systematic, your conversion rate can reach well over 50 percent. As you gain experience, you can achieve well over 75 percent.

MEETING WITH PROSPECTS

CHALLENGE:

I have a good prospect list, but how do I deepen my relationship with them to create a demand for my services?

STANDARD SUGGESTION:

Make phone calls and send emails until they agree to meet you. Don't give up.

BETTER SUGGESTION:

Build a relationship based on your ability to provide information they want.

To get started, you need the right information, which everyone is hungry for. Being the person who can provide that sets you apart from those who are just trying to sell a product. After I decided to focus on restricted stock needs, my partner and I researched and developed distribution lists of executives in our target industries. We were part of the Bear Stearns' network, so every time the Bear Stearns' healthcare analyst released an industry report, we would send it to the healthcare executives on our list. We did the same for those in the technology and telecom fields. We kept ourselves in people's awareness by providing them with actionable information. We didn't just make random phone calls that interrupted their day. We became the team that provided information they wanted and needed, so they looked forward to our contacts. Not only did we send good material on their industries, but we called them every month. At some point, we would ask if what they were receiving was helpful, and if so, we asked for a meeting.

BETTER SUGGESTION:

Build a relationship by providing services they can't get elsewhere and making them feel special.

In addition to research reports, Bear Stearns offered targeted conferences in New York: a healthcare conference, a telecommunications conference, a technology conference, and others. High-profile members of the largest firms in the targeted professions would receive invitations, but there were hundreds, maybe thousands, of others who could benefit from the conference but who weren't invited. My partner and I called on these smaller company executives, who weren't invited to participate in the conference, and invited them to accompany us. We would have private meetings and attend the event with them, which gave them a chance to listen to senior professionals speak and present at the conference. By giving them access to what the best minds in their industries were thinking, and allowing them to mingle, we provided value-added service over and above anything they would expect from their financial advisor. Some of these executives are my clients to this day.

STANDARD SUGGESTION:

Host seminars and lunch investment meetings.

BETTER SUGGESTION:

Host small, intimate educational events.

When people start out in this business, they are often told to prospect by canvassing specific zip codes. They are encouraged to send out blanket mailers to everyone in the area, inviting them to a lunch and/or seminar. From November through March, I must receive four mailers per week from wirehouse advisors, who are probably my competition. They are all asking if I'll go for lunch to learn about their strategies. To me, all this does is diminish their brand. If they are sending *me* mailers, they are not doing their homework. I even had one of those wirehouse advisors leave his business card on my car window at the airport with a note saying, "With a beautiful car like this you must be buying some good dividend-paying stocks. Call me." Now, that is *really* watering down the brand!

THE KEY TO GETTING PEOPLE TO YOUR EVENTS IS TO MAKE THEM INTERESTING

I'm sure that kind of scattershot marketing effort can work for some—but in my opinion it doesn't make the advisor stand out from the pack. Advisors who want to attract wealthy clients need to offer elite service and need to be selective. They don't want to give the impression that they are desperate and will take on anyone with a pulse living in a certain zip code. Elite advisors run their practices like an exclusive country club that is picky about whom it lets in.

This doesn't mean you should never have a mail campaign. Mail campaigns have their place. But they need to be ultra-targeted so you are only reaching the prospects you want in your practice. The more homework you do on your target market and the more specific you make that market, the more success you will have. I know an advisor who runs a practice that provides valuable information to CPAs. These professionals all need continuing education credits to keep their licenses and certifications up to date. Knowing this, the advisor has monthly gourmet lunches, where a speaker provides information that qualifies for continuing education credit. The CPAs come to the lunches for two reasons. They are earning continuing education credits that they need in their practice, and they are receiving a great lunch. So, who do you think these CPAs refer most of their clients to? Exactly! The advisor who is adding value for them. Almost all of this producer's clients live in his moderate-cost-of-living state, yet his team is one of the largest in the country. He has developed a built-in network of referrals by thinking outside the box to produce a value-added service for professionals who can help leverage the business.

The key to getting people to your events is to make them interesting. I know that is easier said than done, but think outside the box. Every event doesn't have to be focused on investments. I host intimate events that focus on providing information people want and need.

I recently hosted an event where I brought in the head of cybersecurity at my firm. I invited clients and prospects who might be interested. I even told clients to bring a friend. The event had nothing to do with investing, but cybersecurity is extremely topical, and the room was full. At one point, the speaker had everyone pull out their cell phones, and right then and there he showed how easily they could be hacked. People came away with five tips on how to make everything they do safer, so that they don't get their identities stolen.

I also sponsored a talk at a local private high school, aimed at parents, on what is involved in the college application process. The speakers I brought in had been on the admissions boards at top universities, but now travel around the country outlining what parents need to do to navigate the process. This is a private college prep school, so everyone was keenly interested in this presentation sponsored by Sal Tiano, J.P. Morgan Securities. I was not asking anybody for business. I was, instead, educating them about something that interests them. Some followed up to speak with me about the event and wanted to learn more about my financial planning business.

Other events of mine have featured speakers for retirees, such as producing safe income investments in a low interest rate environment. After each event, I follow up. "Did you learn anything from it? Is there anything I can do to help you? Would you like to speak to the person directly? Can we sit down and take a look at your existing portfolio? Maybe I can give you a second opinion on some of the things you're doing."

These topical events are my bread and butter. I generally don't sponsor as many investment-related gatherings, unless they are very relevant. The one exception is the event I host in January or February, just after J.P. Morgan comes out with its top themes for the year. We call the meeting a "Guide to the Market." We'll sit down, and we'll just have a discussion. I'll bring a few experts in, and I'll give my own opinion, as well. Afterward, I follow up with everyone who attended.

BETTER SUGGESTION:

Host fun events that allow you and the prospects to get to know one another better.

In addition to these educational events, fun events can be held to build rapport. These can be very small and intimate, such as a golf outing or an afternoon at the ball park, for your top-tier prospects, or they can be larger and include all of your clients, current prospects, and possible prospects, as well as friends and family. I encourage my clients to bring others they think I should get to know to these events.

Any event that brings people together will work. I've rented suites for hockey, football, baseball, tennis, and basketball games and tournaments, as well as golf and equestrian events and concerts. We have done skeet shooting, wine tasting, and wine and whiskey gatherings, and each year, we have a party for the Palm Beach Boat Parade, which passes our house.

The best events, however, are from the heart. Every year, my family and I host a "Holiday Party with a Purpose" to benefit Toys for Tots or Place of Hope, a local foster home community, where we met our foster son.

Depending on the size of the event, we invite friends, families, clients, business associates, centers of influence, and anyone else who might be interested. During the festivities, I make my rounds and mingle. I'm not selling at these events. In fact, obtaining new clients isn't even a priority at these events. I'm building rapport and relationships. It is at these events that I pick up a lot of business without ever even expecting it.

The key to a productive event is to make sure everyone is in a relatively small area so they can talk and interact. A day at a waterpark would certainly attract people, but you'd never be able to find them. Instead, try wine tasting in your living room. A tailgate at a local college game. A barbecue at a nearby microbrewery. The possibilities are only limited by your imagination.

BETTER SUGGESTION:

Leverage other experts.

New advisors might not have the money to fund a large gathering, but there are other ways they can get in front of an audience:

- Take advantage of the wholesalers covering your area. Local advisors are a wholesaler's target audience. The fund business is a very competitive one, and every mutual fund and money management firm has a marketing budget specifically geared to help local advisors educate their clients and prospects. Wholesalers will even help bring in speakers, and they have a lot of experience with these events. Use them!

- Add value to wholesaler events by having an estate planning attorney or a tax accountant speak. If these professionals are part of the advisor's networking group, even better. If they work for a large wirehouse, they can bring in other experts from their firm. These experts are paid to help, so take advantage of that.

- Of course, advisors should also speak at these events to help the audience get to know them. These aren't large events, but they are a good way to get a foot in the door on someone else's dime.

- When you call to invite a prospect, ask the person to bring someone else who might be interested. Make sure to follow up the day before the event to confirm attendance. Then do as much due diligence as possible on every person attending.

FOLLOWING UP AFTER MEETING WITH A PROSPECT

Whether you meet someone at an event, receive an introduction, or garner a referral, follow up on a consistent, systematic basis.

CHALLENGE:

How do I get a prospect to take my calls or return my emails?

STANDARD SUGGESTION:

Be persistent. Just keep calling and emailing.

BETTER SUGGESTION:

Provide them with information so they look forward to your follow-up calls and emails.

The purpose of all of these connections is to keep you, the rainmaker, in front of your prospects, of course. But it is more than that. It is to reframe your image from salesperson to advisor and solution provider. You want the prospects to look forward to the calls and emails because they are providing useful information.

Staying in contact with prospects does not need to involve long conversations. Let the prospects take the lead. If they are willing to talk, listen and move the conversation forward. Here are some ideas you might want to try:

- If you come across a book or magazine article that you think one of your prospects would like, send it to their office with a handwritten note. "Hi, Mary. When we spoke last week, you mentioned that you were taking a golf vacation in the Caribbean. I just came across this article in *Golf Digest* on the top ten courses in the Caribbean. I thought you might find it interesting. Looking forward to talking to you when you get back and hearing all about your trip."

- Set up Google Alerts systems for your prospects. Whenever they or their companies are mentioned in the news, you'll receive an alert. Send a quick text, email, or note with the appropriate reaction to the news. I have done this for years, and I can tell you firsthand that prospects and clients are impressed when they know you follow their interests and show that you care.

- I like to have a photographer at some of the events I hold. One great way to follow up is to send a picture of your prospect/ client (with spouse is a plus) with a short, handwritten note from the event. It can be as simple as, "John and Julie, I thought you would like to see this great photo from the other night. I hope you had as much fun as I did."

These little touches tell clients and prospects that they are viewed as individuals, not just business associates.

BETTER SUGGESTION:

Use a good CRM program to capture information on the prospect and keep your follow-up efforts systematic.

I've found that the best way to stay organized and keep things from falling through the cracks is to use a good CRM program. As soon as I have a new prospect name, I enter it in the program with details on how we met, what I know about the person, and any other information that will help me develop a relationship. I set the reminder feature to follow up two weeks later.

For example, if I connect with fifteen new prospects, I'll set each of their reminders for two weeks in the future, with five on Tuesday, five on Wednesday, and five on Thursday. Then every time I speak to them, I will take notes and use information from that conversation to build a deeper relationship. I'll enter those notes in the CRM program to pull up when I contact them next. Every member of my team can see the notes, so we are all completely informed. I'm not trying to sell my prospects anything at this point. In fact, I'm never selling products. The goal is to get these prospects to be a "buyer" of you, your team, and your firm. I want to become their partner in growing and protecting their wealth.

Before I leave for the day, I use the system to print out the clients/ prospects I need to reach the next day, how I want to reach them, and what I want to say. That way, I know what to do the second I

ORGANIZATION WITH A PURPOSE IS KEY

walk into my office, so there is no wasted time.

I use multiple ways to connect—handwritten notes (very few people spend the time to write handwritten notes anymore, so those of us who do really stand out), emails, and phone calls. If I know the prospect well, I even use text for a quick "Have you seen this?" note.

But I'm not just ticking tasks off a checklist. There is a reason behind each activity. Organization with a purpose is key.

BETTER SUGGESTION:

Be memorable.

To improve the odds of prospects taking a rainmaker's calls, they have to remember who you are. Just as becoming an expert sets an advisor apart, doing the unexpected will keep you in the forefront of your prospects' minds. Here are a couple of ideas to get started:

ALWAYS DRESS APPROPRIATELY

Today, there is a trend to dress down in casual attire. To me, casual dress means casual business. Depending on the part of the country in which your office is located and the type of client/prospect you are visiting, appropriate dress might not always mean a business suit. However, I would always rather be overdressed than underdressed. Being dressed appropriately doesn't mean you can't have fun. I like to wear very distinctive ties, which serve the dual purpose of making me feel appropriately dressed while also being memorable. I once visited a CEO who commented that he loved my tie. A few months later, I had the tie company make a similar tie with his company's logo on it and sent it to him. It was a totally unexpected gesture, and he was delighted. A few weeks later, he called me to let me know he was going to be interviewed on CNBC that afternoon, and he wanted me to watch. During the interview, he wore the tie I gave him. He told me he had so many comments about the tie from his employees that he asked if I could get him a few more so he could give them to his board. I was able do that, and he gave one to every board member at the next board meeting[7]. Eventually, I ended up doing business with all the top executives and several board members at that firm. This became a Fortune 100 company, so it was quite a bit of business. Obviously, to keep the business and grow it, you have to be good at what you do and add value. The CEO could vouch that my team and I would add value. But the tie was the hook that got the others to discover who I was in the first place! It is the little things that show you care and go above and beyond that will get others to give you a chance.

BE A GREAT STORYTELLER

Being a storyteller is a great way to attract an audience. You don't want to talk too much—prospects will get very bored very quickly if you don't also listen to them—but everyone loves a good story.

Some people seem to have the gift of gab from the time they can put two words together, but storytelling is a skill that can be learned. Get online and study TED talks. Pick up tips from listening to and watching those who tell good stories. (A lot of good storytelling comes from facial expressions and body language.) Think about joining Toastmasters International (www.toastmasters.org). Some of the best storytellers I know learned by joining an improv group. They had a great time and honed an invaluable skill. Keep your eyes open for situations that lend themselves to stories. If you are unsure of

---

7   Make sure you adhere to your firm's gift policy before giving anything to clients or prospects.

yourself, practice by recording stories on your phone until you are happy with the presentation and the material. The more confident you are, the better you'll come across. Entertaining people with your stories will soon be second nature and will certainly make you memorable.

Once the groundwork has been laid and you have developed a relationship with prospects, it's time to meet and offer a proposal.

CONVERTING PROSPECTS INTO CLIENTS

CHALLENGE:

How do I convert a prospect into a client?

STANDARD SUGGESTION:

Send all your prospects data showing the best performing funds you or your company are suggesting to clients. Tell them you could do the same for them.

BETTER SUGGESTION:

Build a relationship with your prospects, as well as with those around them.

Early in my career, I was calling on a prospect of considerable net worth. I had done my homework and believed that I could offer him better and more personal service than he was getting from his current advisor. I called his office at least once a month, and sometimes once a week, for two years. Every few months he'd take my call, and we'd talk about a variety of things, not always business related. But most days, he was too busy to get on the line. During this time, however, I developed a very good rapport with his personal assistant. I made it abundantly clear that my ultimate goal was to do business with her boss, but on the days when he wasn't available, she and I would chat for a bit. When I found out her mother passed away, I sent a handwritten note. When her child was born, I sent a gift. I wasn't just cold-calling the next name on a list—I was building a relationship with another human being.

One day, after two years of regular calling, she answered the phone and told me that she had overheard her boss complaining about his existing advisor. She went on to tell me that he would be working late the following Wednesday. She suggested that if I called him at 6:15 p.m., he would pick up, because she was leaving at 6:00 p.m. I did. He did. And the result was he has become one of my largest clients over the past twenty years.

This is what rainmaking is all about. It's not smiling and dialing (though phone calling can play a part). It's not harassing people. It's investing the time and energy, with common decency and courtesy, to develop a relationship. In this case, I got to know the assistant before I connected with the prospect. In other cases, I get to know the prospect directly. In all cases, I treat my prospects as the individual people they are, not as just names on a list.

Some might think that converting this prospect was luck. After all, if he hadn't been unhappy with his current advisor, he might not ever have talked to me. But we make our own luck. Yes, he was unhappy, which gave me an opening. But I had positioned myself to take advantage of the opening. Without a game plan that kept me professionally persistent, I would not have been prepared when the opportunity arrived. I can cite several examples like this over the past twenty years, so what was true decades ago is still true today.

BETTER SUGGESTION:

Establish a need.

The greatest hindrance to closing a deal is indifference. If prospects do not care about what you have to offer, they won't make any effort to learn more. You need to give people a reason to engage. These are some of the ways I've found that work well:

- Prospects and clients don't care how much you know until they know how much you care. That means advisors need to approach prospecting for new clients in the same way they would approach making new friends. You want to get to know them and show an interest in them personally. Try to solve a problem for them, just because you can. Maybe introduce them to someone who enjoys the same hobby. Maybe suggest a good place to fish. It doesn't have to be a big problem or a big solution. It only needs to let them know that you have listened to them. When you do that, they will want to respond and give you a chance to show them what else you can help them with.

- Once prospects sit down and show you their portfolio, input their current securities into your system. That way, you will be notified whenever one of those securities is mentioned in the news or analysts' reports. You can get alerts from Bloomberg, your own system, or even Google. If your firm publishes proprietary research, that is even better.

For example, if prospect Joe Smith has a large position in Bristol-Myers and the company reports earnings, I will show him what our firm reports. I don't overwhelm his email box, but there is no reason not to send a quick note. "Just want to let you know our analyst came out with these comments on Bristol-Myers' earnings. Thought you'd find this interesting."

I like to send these e-mails at 7:15 in the morning when their other advisor is sleeping but I'm in the office listening to our research call. I'm basically asking, "What does your existing advisor say about the Bristol-Myers report?" knowing that their current advisor probably hasn't said anything. Giving prospects a chance to see that there really is a difference between advisors provides them with a reason to consider working with you.

The absolute best time to convert prospects into new clients is during a bear market or when one of their largest positions declines substantially. When the latter happens, I will often call a prospect and ask, "What is Merrill saying about the security?" Or even better, if I see that Merrill downgraded the security, I will often call the prospect and ask what their current advisor is saying about the position since it has been downgraded. I am sorry to say that the average advisor is inherently lazy and will typically not even notify their clients when a position is downgraded. Or they will sadly not know themselves because they have not been paying attention to their firm's research. The same can be said about bear markets. Many advisors avoid speaking to their clients when there is bad news. However, this is exactly the time to communicate with them more.

The idea of these calls is not to embarrass a prospect's current advisors, but to show the prospect the type of service one should be expecting. If the current advisor is giving a high level of service, the prospect will probably stay right there. But if my phone calls show that there's a better way, the prospect will typically be open to doing business.

CHALLENGE:

How do I get a face-to-face business meeting?

STANDARD SUGGESTION:

Go down your list and email each prospect with an offer to meet for lunch. You can slowly work your way to asking for their business while enjoying a nice sandwich.

BETTER SUGGESTION:

Be straightforward and transparent. Just ask.

Once I have qualified a prospect and we've reached the stage that it makes sense to meet in person to discuss business, I will call or send an email.

If I'm just following up on a meeting or providing information, I will send an email and say, "Thanks for taking the time to meet with me. I'll follow up in a week or two." I then do so using a combination of methods. One week, I may send a handwritten note. Another week, I may craft an email. Another week, I'll pick up the phone and call. But I always try to use the phone to make an appointment when I want to have a meeting.

When you call, be straightforward. Be clear. Now is not the time to be coy. The fact is, it's refreshing for busy people when people come straight out and ask for what they want. "We talked a bit at the cybersecurity event. Let's set up a meeting where we can look at your portfolio and see if it makes sense for us to work together. If it makes sense and we can help you, great. If not, I met a new friend. No pressure. At this point in my career, I like to do business with the right fit."

If prospects don't respond to my initial calls or emails, I'll put them on my call-again list to circle back in a week or two. Then, if they don't return my messages the second time in two weeks, I'll send an email, saying, "I've reached out to you a couple of times. I know you might be busy. Let's set up a time when we can discuss how I may be able to further assist you."

After several tries, I'm not afraid to say, "I just want to let you know I've reached out to you a few times. If you're not interested, let me know. I won't bug you anymore. But if you are interested, let me know a better time to communicate with you, because I don't want to waste your time or mine."

A lot of people beat around the bush. They say, "Let's get together," and they have lunch, but they're afraid to ask for the business. I tell prospects up front, "Here's what I'd like to do at our next meeting. I want to find out a little bit more about what you do, how I might be able to service you in the future, and whether we're a good fit. If it's a good fit, we'll take the next step. I'll ask you for some information. Everything we discuss will be confidential, and if it's not a good fit, then you know what? All I ask is that if you think what I do is educational and helpful, keep me in mind for someone who fits our business model who would appreciate what we do for our clients." It's totally nonthreatening.

CHALLENGE:

What action steps should I take at the prospect meetings?

STANDARD SUGGESTION:

Have a proposed portfolio allocation ready to show. This will give you something concrete to talk about.

BETTER SUGGESTION:

Speak less, listen more, and ask open-ended questions.

The first formal meeting with a prospect should involve time to go over the prospect's current portfolio. It is difficult to prepare a dedicated proposal if you don't know details about what the prospect is already doing.

Before we get into the portfolio, however, I like to spend the first twenty minutes asking about a prospect's outside interests. Most successful people like to speak about their families. And they like to talk about their businesses and how they made their wealth. We talk about where they went to school, their hobbies, and what they like to do in their spare time. Once we have relaxed and developed a rapport, I transition into their portfolios.

The first thing I look for is what they like about their portfolio. Everyone likes to talk about the positive. Then I ask what they wish they had done better. What are their financial goals for the future? What keeps them up at night? Do they have a family Investment Policy Statement? Do both spouses make the decisions jointly? Are they on the same page? I often find that one spouse is more conservative than the other. In that case, how do we navigate those differences? If something happened to them, would they be confident that their spouse or family members would carry out the plan? Are they interested in educating the next generation about the wealth that was created? Usually the prospect will open up when you ask questions like these.

At the end of the meeting, let them know that you and your firm handle families just like theirs (only if it is true, of course). Let them know their assets will be safe with your firm or where you custody their assets. Be brief. Be succinct. Be confident.

Then tell your prospect how you would like to move forward. Say that you would like to invest the time to do a full-fledged financial plan, including an optimal asset allocation and cash flow analysis. Explain that there will be no charge, and all you ask is that if the proposal is impressive and useful, the prospect will consider using you and your firm. I always end by asking, "Does that sound reasonable?"

More times than not, the prospect answers in the affirmative. Take some time to answer any questions and let the person know that you will take no more than three to five business days to prepare the proposal. Then set up the second meeting to present it in person.

Although my goal is not to convert the prospect at the first meeting (it is to get a full picture of the financial objectives and connect personally), it does happen on occasion. However, prospects will normally wait for the proposal at the second meeting. It is at this second meeting that I continue to build rapport and trust and then ask them to partner with me and my team in growing and protecting their wealth.

When we reach the proposal stage, I keep it simple, but detailed. I know that sounds like an oxymoron, but it's not. *Simple* means it's logical, practical, and actionable. There are no unnecessary twists and turns. *Detailed* means I fill in all the blanks, so the prospect isn't left wondering what I'm doing and why.

Each proposal involves a similar process:

1. Start off with an analysis of the prospect's existing portfolio. Be careful not to rip the current portfolio apart. Some of it will very likely be decent, and a new advisor will gain credibility by pointing out what is good. People don't want to think they've been doing it all wrong for years. I recently met with a new client who had his portfolio at a large regional bank. The bank's overall investment performance had been horrible. However, his fixed-income assets were very good and very high quality. I had no interest in changing them, which I told him. He really appreciated my honesty, and he left the meeting knowing he could trust me to always tell him the truth.

2. Provide a comprehensive wealth management plan. Based on earlier conversations you've had with the prospect, you should be able to provide a comprehensive plan that takes into account the risk-return profile and current assets and cash flow, as well as current and future liabilities. This plan could also include recommendations on titling assets, creating trusts, gifting, and other strategies for minimizing taxes and risk, while maximizing returns. Your firm likely has a good software program that will help you generate this plan.

3. Explain how you plan to transition the current portfolio to one you recommend.

    Point out exactly what assets you think need to be replaced and how. Let the prospect know that a complete transition can take a year or more, because investors need to be aware of the tax implications involved in selling a large amount of securities—if that's what you are doing. If you are dealing with a new client who has deposited cash with you rather than transferred a portfolio of securities, the timing is much easier to predict. I don't believe in sitting on cash. I believe it should be working for you. So, I invest cash deposits very quickly into the appropriate portfolio of equities and fixed-income assets.

4. Make sure the client knows exactly what kind of service to expect from you and your team.

    This is where you can really set yourself apart. How often will you be in touch? How often do you expect to meet in person? The more specific you can be, the better.

5. Explain exactly what your services will cost.

    Do not hide anything. Many advisors will tell the client the advisor fee but leave out any fees required by third-party managers or mutual funds. Make sure you disclose any and all fees, including any underlying expenses of the investments. You are looking to build a trusting, long-term relationship. Hiding some of the costs will never end well.

    Our total fees are almost always comparable to the total fees of others. But we are transparent and honest from the beginning, which has earned us many clients over the years.

GETTING TO "YES"

Before each meeting, I always know what my goal is, and I'm not afraid to ask for information. It might be to see the current portfolio; it might be to nail down goals; or it might be a request to turn part of the portfolio over. In any case, I ask. Don't be afraid to be direct. Wealthy people appreciate it, and they will see you as the professional you are.

However, when it comes time to ask for their business, I don't just sit down and say, "Do you want to hire me?" As we go through the process outlined previously, I will ask questions that naturally elicit an answer of yes:

"Does that make sense?" Yes.

"Does that seem reasonable?" Yes.

"Is this something you'd like to do?" Yes.

Each time a prospect says yes, it makes it easier to say yes again. Each "yes" builds rapport and reinforces that you are on the same side of the table. You are becoming a team.

At the end of the meeting, ask for the business: "I am highly confident we can make a positive impact for you and your family. I'd like to work with you … OK?"

Then be quiet. You are asking for the business. Do not be the next person to speak. By the time you get to this final question, "Would you like to work together?" the prospect should be ready and willing to say, "Yes!"

A FEW CAUTIONS

When it comes to rainmaking, I have made it a habit never to prospect where I live and play. Clients will often become friends, but friends don't necessarily become clients.

When I was first starting out, I joined a country club that was offering a great deal for young members. One day, I was playing golf with a group of friends at the club. We saw another guy walking our way and the others in my group started to chuckle and roll their eyes. They said, "Here comes Harry Jones. Make sure you cover your pockets. He's going to try to get in them." I didn't understand what they meant at first, but later they told me that Harry was an insurance salesman. His job was to play golf every day and try to get you to buy insurance from him. No one wanted to be his friend because they all knew they were only prospects to him.

Don't be Harry Jones. You want friends and acquaintances to be at ease around you. You don't want them to feel that they have to avoid you in the local grocery store because they aren't doing business with you. Now, I actually do a lot of business where I live and play. But it's only from people who have approached me. And, strategically, I've done that on purpose. I want people to trust me and my motives. I want to position myself so that they want to come to me. You can almost see the relief on their faces that I'm not chasing after them.

It's not difficult to separate my personal life from my business life. For example, my wife and I often find ourselves playing golf on the same afternoons, and our respective groups sometimes meet up afterward for drinks and dinner. During these dinners, I've often had someone ask me, "Do you do business with so and so?"

And I'll say, "You'll have to ask them. I'm not at liberty to discuss that." And if somebody ever wants to bring up business with me when we're having a social outing, I simply say, "My office is the time and the place for that. So, feel free to call me. Here's my office number." I'll bring up business in small talk with people, but when it comes to real business, I keep it separate from the rest of my life.

There are times, however, when you know a good social connection could be a decent client. The way to bring up business in an unthreatening way is to keep it simple and be direct. Invariably some of your social connections will ask you (hopefully in private) some questions about your career or job. The way I bridge the gap is simple: "John, your friendship to me is way more important than ever doing business together. You know what I do … if there is ever a time you would like discuss anything with me—financial planning, estate planning, a second opinion on an alternative investment, the right asset allocation, or whatever is on your mind—let me know and don't consider it an imposition. I'd be happy to help with no strings attached."

I remember two specific social connections who became clients with those words. One said he thought I had a closed practice and wasn't taking on any more clients because I never asked him or my other friends for business. I had a similar conversation with another friend (after she brought up something in her financial life), who told me she would love to work with me but thought my minimums were much higher than what she had to invest (and she had over $10 million). So, when I say that I don't mix the social aspects of my life with the professional, I don't mean that I never talk business with friends. What I mean is that I don't chase them. But if business matters come up organically, I follow them where they lead. After breaking the ice and doing well for friends, you know what will follow—many unsolicited referrals.

GUARD YOUR BRAND

When executing a game plan, be aware of the brand image you are projecting. One of the goals of a game plan is to articulate your brand so that you can frame yourself in your clients' and prospects' minds. I want to be seen as a value and a bargain. That doesn't mean I'm cheap. It means I provide such high-end, value-added service that my team's compensation is seen as a bargain.

You need to be able to articulate your brand in a one- or two-sentence mission statement. If you can't put it into words, then you really don't know what you want to be. And if *you* don't know, how will anyone else? When we get into the chapter on building a team, I'll talk more about how important it is that everyone on the team knows and understands the mission statement, but for now, just know—you need to have one!

BE SELECTIVE

When you are building your prospect list, it can be tempting to take on anyone and everyone. This is a mistake if you are building an elite practice. You have to know the type of client that works with your practice and stick to that type. If someone wants to day trade, or they need weekly personal calls and hand-holding, or they want to do something that I can't handle, then we won't pursue them. Nothing good ever comes from failing to deliver.

People often ask if I have minimums. I actually do have a minimum for new clients, unless they are referrals or family members of current clients. But I can be flexible. I'm at a point in my career where I want to do business only with good people. That is really more important to me than a minimum account size. If a prospect fits in line with what we can do well, I might decide to take that person on, even if the funds don't meet my stated minimum.

A lot of advisors will have a $5 million or $10 million minimum, and they won't budge. That means that if their $50 million client comes to them and says, "My nephew would like to open an account with $1 million," they will turn them down, because that nephew doesn't meet the minimum. The nephew will then go to someone else and could have a great experience with the other firm. Next thing you know, your big client is leaving for the firm his nephew can't stop talking about.

Now, I don't take everybody, even if they are nice or related to my largest client. But when I turn people away, it's because I won't be able to service them correctly, and I'll have to charge too much. If that happens, I'll say, "I don't think I'm right for you. However, I will help you start off with the right asset allocation model, and I'll refer you to somebody who I think makes sense. Or you can go to Fidelity, and I'll help you pick the funds. We can still talk once a year and see how things are going, but I don't want to overcharge you for something you don't need."

This approach works very well for prospects who aren't quite ready to make the commitment needed to benefit from our practice at this time but might be in the future. For example, there was one couple that was interested in working with us, but they had two children in college and needed to keep their assets liquid to pay for tuition. We all agreed this wasn't the right time for them to invest with me. But I gave them some asset allocation ideas, and we have kept in touch. After their children graduate and the parents are able to place more of their assets in longer-term investments, I expect the couple will come on as a formal client.

KEY TAKEAWAYS

- Host events to build relationships with prospects.

- Know what makes your practice different and be able to articulate it.

- Be direct—ask for what you want.

- Keep it human.

CHAPTER 5
USING STRUCTURAL ALPHA TO BECOME INDISPENSABLE

I HAVE A VERY WEALTHY client who has been with me for many years. We've become close friends and have spent many occasions together. I've seen him through his wife's passing, as well as his own health problems. I've supported him both as a good friend and as a good professional. For example, despite his health scare about ten years ago, I was able to put him in contact with an insurance agent who helped him secure a substantial life insurance policy.

I also introduced him to a great estate planning attorney, who worked with him to make sure his affairs were in order, just in case. He came to me recently to tell me he was getting ready to retire and wanted to make whatever changes were needed in his financial plan to do that. We went through a cash flow analysis and what he could expect in retirement. We used tax-advantaged gifting techniques to move money into trusts. We adjusted portfolios to provide the income he would need. With all the details taken care of, he was really excited to enter the next phase of his life.

Just a few weeks later, he called me. "You're my first phone call," he said. "I just came from the doctor and I have terminal cancer. I'm not ready to tell my kids yet, but I thought I could call you." I didn't know what to say, so I just listened, the same way I'd listened to him whenever we had talked over the years. During that forty-five-minute call, he talked about what he was feeling, but he also thanked me for introducing him to the insurance agent who had secured a policy large enough to pay the estate taxes and make sure his kids were set. I told him we needed to hope for the best but plan for the worst, and a large part of that plan was to educate his children on investing and protecting the wealth they would inherit from his estate. I'd seen the kids grow up and had been involved with their lives, but we hadn't started to talk to them about managing wealth because of their younger ages. That need had seemed to be far in the future.

When my client/friend is ready to tell his kids, I am confident that he will let them know that I have helped him manage his wealth and what that involves. "This is the guy who made sure I had insurance. Who made sure I had an estate plan in gear. And he's going to educate you on what to do and how to structure things so that when I'm gone, you're comfortable."

I hope that client lives another twenty years, but based on his recent diagnosis, that's very unlikely. But whether it's next year or twenty years from now, I know that my team and I will be working with the next generation long after he's gone, because I'm not just focused on numbers—I'm focused on people.

Too many advisors focus on bringing in new clients and forget that it is the current clients who provide the foundation for the business. Once a prospect becomes a client, the real work begins. It's really not that difficult to keep your existing clients happy, and it has nothing to do with beating benchmarks. A top advisor has already built a foundation for trust, and now they just need to deliver.

An elite advisor should have three primary goals:

1. to be a client's only or lead advisor (i.e., their CFO),

2. to be a trusted source of knowledge, and

3. to have wealthy clients refer more like them.

To accomplish these goals, advisors need more than an excellent investment track record. They need to provide Four Seasons-like service and Amazon-like efficiency. In other words, they must surround clients with structural alpha.

To review, structural alpha is the value we create in our clients' lives from our advice on better ways to structure, organize, and plan for their family needs and goals. It is a *systematic, methodical approach* that enables you and your team to be indispensable in the eyes of your clients. You aren't just a finance resource; you are a total problem-solving resource.

That's structural alpha. It is being so connected to your clients that they no longer see you as a financial advisor; they see you as a trusted friend who knows the best people and resources and can help in any situation. I want to be an advisor who cannot be easily replaced. I'm a confidant who will be in their lives and their children's lives for decades.

PUTTING STRUCTURAL ALPHA INTO PRACTICE

When we use the term *alpha* in the marketplace, we mean performance above and beyond a benchmark. *Structural alpha* is similar in that it means you have a structure in place that allows you to systematically provide service over and above what is expected.

Structural alpha has three main components:

1. Treat your clients like family and stay in regular contact with them.

2. Become a fountain of knowledge.

3. Have a program to educate the clients and their families. And do all of it in a methodical, systematic manner.

COMMUNICATION AND TREATING YOUR CLIENTS LIKE FAMILY

My clients are an extension of my family. Many advisors see their role simply as providing investment products. This is a very short-sighted strategy. Why should any client remain with you if all you are doing is providing a service that thousands of other advisors can provide?

Instead, if you want to retain clients for decades, communicate with them as effectively as possible, and treat them like family.

HAVE A STRONG BUSINESS MANAGEMENT SYSTEM IN PLACE

There is no way you can be systematic about providing structural alpha—superior service in a methodical, systematic way—without everyone in your office religiously using an excellent customer relationship management (CRM) system. Data is powerful, and being systematic in how you collect and use it can make the difference between having a book of clients who might leave at any moment and having a book of loyal clients who expect to stay with you long term.

I've developed some very specific procedures to take full advantage of our CRM program and use it to enhance my structural alpha system.

COLLECT AS MUCH DATA AS POSSIBLE

First of all, set up several pages in the CRM software for each client. On the first page, set up fields to capture the name of the primary contact and all contact information—addresses for home, work, and vacation spots; phone numbers for landlines and mobiles; email for home and work. This section should indicate the preferred method of contact. Some clients like text messages, but you have to be careful what information you distribute via text because it isn't regulated or secure.

Have a section for the spouse that contains the same information. Many advisors stop here, but elite advisors will add a section for children and grandchildren, as well as other close relatives, such as the client's parents. This section should include birthdays, where the children/relatives live, where they go to school, and any other information that will help you build a relationship with the client.

I also include a field that explains how the client became a prospect, whether it was the result of an event or a referral from a client or professional contact. In addition, I'll note which other clients or prospects the person may know.

On the next page, I list all the client's key contacts. These include the client's CPA and attorney, physician, real estate agent, and other professionals the client deals with on a regular basis. I have a section for other bank accounts and any retirement plans, such as a 401(k), that are in place. Make sure to include a field for tax brackets.

I also include a section on the client's employer. I want to know if the company is publicly traded, what its stock symbol is, how many shares are outstanding, and what size stake the client has in it. All of this information will help me track the firm and connect with the client when something pops up in my notification system.

Then I have a page called "preferences." Every conversation that my team has with the family or the primary contact is a new opportunity to find out more information. What are their food likes? What are their favorite restaurants? Do they have any allergies? How do they like their coffee if they come into the office? Do they prefer tea or water? Are they on any boards? What sports teams do they like? Do they play sports? Which schools did they attend? What is their religion? What are their political beliefs? (I don't talk about religion and politics too often with clients, but it's nice to know if you can find out tidbits about their affiliations.) What other interests do they have? What are their favorite vacation spots? What charities are they involved with? You get the idea.

The goal is to find out as much information as possible, so our connections are conversational, not sterile. For instance, if my assistant speaks with a client about a monthly distribution, they will also talk about the client's plans for the weekend. She will then enter that conversation in the CRM program, so if someone else in the office were to connect with the client in the next week, anyone could refer to the weekend plans and ask how things went. This attention to the details of their lives lets clients know that we see them as more than just names in our book.

This page is also where I note the appropriate distribution lists. I have approximately twenty lists. If the client is an executive, for example, I will place that person's name on our research list. Some clients enjoy technology research. Others appreciate macroeconomics. Still others may prefer research on the general market, which our firm publishes quite often. So, I will check off the appropriate lists.

Having these lists means I can quickly email relevant information to clients and very easily keep in touch on a regular basis.

SET UP A CONSISTENT CONTACT SCHEDULE

The advantage of a CRM system is that it keeps me on track to contact clients on a regular basis. Using their preferences, I set up a schedule for each client. Some clients like to be called weekly, so I may call them every Wednesday. I'll do that for six months, then change it to another day just so it doesn't feel so scripted. I touch base with most clients monthly, though some are every other month and others once per quarter. I try to balance it so that I have a similar number of contacts to make each day. And it is me making the contacts. I personally contact each client every time.

Before I leave the office each night, I print my "recall list" for the next day. Typically, there are about ten people that I need to call, just to check in with them. I don't leave my desk until I call and either speak to or leave a message for everyone on my list. If I have to leave a message, I'll set the CRM to remind me to reach out in a couple of days via email if I haven't heard back from them.

Everybody on our team takes notes and enters them into the system every single time they communicate in any way with a client or a prospect. Everybody can then access that information, and we don't let things slip through the cracks. That's very, very important.

Send articles, statistics, books, etc., on topics you know will interest each client. Send notes on their birthdays, anniversaries, or other celebratory dates. I recently called a lady who just turned ninety-nine to wish her a happy birthday and plan our annual lunch. We met when I was twenty-nine years old, and I've been doing business with her for more than twenty-five years now. I don't think that would have happened, no matter how stellar my investment advice, if I hadn't developed a personal relationship that means she looks forward to our birthday lunch each year.

My team is constantly sending out birthday cards, because we send to clients, spouses, and, sometimes, children. But I also pick up the phone and call on their birthday and say, "Hello. Just wanted to be the first to wish you a happy birthday today. Hope you have a great day."

When our clients are still just prospects, we tell them what they can expect from us when it comes to communicating. We tell them that if they call us anytime during our business hours, between seven and five o'clock, Monday through Friday, they will rarely get voicemail. In fact, their phone calls will typically be answered by the second ring. And they will be answered in a friendly manner. "Good morning, this is Sal." We encourage their incoming calls, but we let them know that we will be calling them on a regular basis, depending on how often they want to connect and their individual circumstances. We also tell them that if there is a major event in the market, we will typically send out an email explaining the event and the impact it will have on investments. Many times, we attach firm research, but clients appreciate it when I summarize the detailed report in a few bullet points in the body of the email. We also tell them that we will typically be in touch with them more in a bear market than a bull market. It is more important to make outgoing phone calls or meetings when the market is going down than when it is going up.

TAKE A GENUINE INTEREST

When you talk to clients, really listen to what they are saying. Are they planning a trip? Are they adopting a new dog? Are they putting an addition on their house or downsizing? Is one of their children graduating from college? Listen to how things are going in their lives and be ready to offer solutions if called for. I remember speaking with a client on our regular monthly chat. He mentioned that he and his son were planning a road trip to visit as many baseball parks as possible. A week later, I sent him a book that covered the history of every major league baseball stadium in the US and Canada. About a month after that, we had our quarterly evaluation meeting, which went very well. At that meeting, the client told me how much he and his son had appreciated the book, and they decided they were going to transfer another substantial account to us. I have no idea whether the book on baseball parks had anything to do with it. But I am guessing that it did.

I have never had a client who didn't appreciate it when I took an interest in his or her children. I start with the basics, such as their names and ambitions. But then I offer more. I'm willing to help them in any way I can. I have written recommendations for college applications and provided job leads, when appropriate. I also often send congratulatory notes if I see that their children or others in the family have done something noteworthy, such as announced an engagement, been accepted to a college, or been named to the board of a local charity.

You will also want to get to know your clients' families, because those families will one day inherit the estate—and you'd like the assets to stay with you and your team rather than be moved to another advisor. Include grown children in your events. Make sure the spouse is treated as an equal partner. Build a relationship with the entire family, not just the main client. A survey by *Investment News* found that 66 percent of children fire their parents' financial advisor after they inherit their parents' wealth.[8] Research also shows that the

---

8   Skinner, "The great wealth transfer is coming, putting advisors at risk."

surviving spouse transfers assets to another advisor 70 percent of the time.[9] Imagine the hit on the business if two-thirds of the best clients disappear.

Heirs aren't moving assets because they don't trust their spouses' or parents' advisors. They are moving those assets because they don't know them! Historically, many advisors have only dealt with the patriarch, who handled the money and the decisions. That is changing as more women and spouses become actively involved in the decision making. However, no matter who the primary decision maker is, you need to get to know the entire family.

Don't be afraid to use the phone. We are living in an email age, but phone calls create a much more intimate connection. I have clients all over the country. I visit some of them less frequently, but I do quarterly reviews with them by phone. I'll also use the phone for my regular weekly, monthly, and quarterly check-ins. It's particularly important to use the phone if you need to deliver bad news, or if there is a problem that needs to be resolved. It just creates a better, more personal relationship than email or text. However, emails work when you need to deliver news quickly to many at once.

ANTICIPATE WORRY AND CALM FEARS

When the Brexit vote was making news in 2016, clients were asking what it meant to them. No one really understood it, and they wondered why the Dow Jones Industrial Average was down 500 points after a vote in England. Whenever something like this happens, our firm typically will host a research call and issue a report explaining what is happening and what it means for investors. By eight thirty that morning, I was able to send an email to all of my clients and prospects explaining why Brexit is not bad for America,

---

9   Polyak, "For some widows, breaking up with an advisor is easy to do."

and why it may have created a great buying opportunity at those prices.

When sending these reports, you want to make it easy for your clients to access the information. In this case, I sent an email to my distribution list saying, "I just got off a conference call. I've attached the report. Let me summarize it for you."

I then took two sentences and a few bullet points to explain the report conclusions very simply and concisely. "Here's what the market is doing. Here are the actions we're taking. By the way, I'm in the trenches with you. I'm a buyer today for my own personal account at the same prices I'm buying for you."

The response to this email was uniformly positive. One email, which I remember specifically, said, "Thank you for summarizing it. I had no idea what Brexit was. You know how to explain things clearly and succinctly. That's what I appreciate about you. You're on the ball."

I received three referrals from sending that email. In addition, I had another client e-mail me, "I never heard from my other advisor. I want to transfer another account to you."

When the world is looking rocky, it's important that you get in front of your clients swiftly and summarize the information in plain English. You would think this would just be standard blocking and tackling, but you'd be surprised at how many advisors don't do it.

Another example: on Monday, February 5, 2018, the Dow closed down 1,175 points—its worst point drop on record.[10] If there was ever a time when an advisor would want to pull the covers over his head and stay in bed, this was it. But instead of avoiding my clients and hoping the market would rebound before I had to talk to them, I proactively reached out to calm the waters. On Tuesday

---

10   Egan, "Dow plunges 1,175—worst point decline in history."

morning, I sent an email to every prospect, every client, every center of influence I knew. Our chief economist put out an excellent piece explaining what was happening, so I attached it saying, "I know you're wondering what is going on with the newfound market volatility. The attached piece does an excellent job of explaining what is happening, and what we can expect going forward. In case you don't have time to open it, I'm going to summarize it. If you have questions about your portfolio, I'm here all day."

No one is happy when things don't go as planned, but you can't let fear of your clients' reactions paralyze you. Just be professional and make that call or set up that meeting. My suggestion is to deliver it as soon as possible and early in the day. If they've unexpectedly lost capital, or if future cash flow projections have changed for the worse, tell them straight out. No euphemisms. No soft pedaling. Let them know what happened, why it happened, and what you are going to do about it. Offering a solution is key. Don't leave clients wondering what they should do next. If you don't have a solution immediately, tell them you will exhaust all possibilities to find one and will be getting back to them as soon as possible. Give them a solution, and they will almost always stick with you and work through the difficulties. Be proactive with bad news and clients will know you are tough enough and honest enough to handle their assets.

Also, your clients should always know they can contact you or your team at any time. One of my clients once reached out to me on a Sunday morning. He was buying a multimillion-dollar property and needed a letter confirming that he had the liquidity to purchase it. If he didn't get the letter right away, he could lose the property. He had assets with a couple of other advisors, but he said, "Sal, you are the only one I felt would answer my call, and could help me, on a Sunday." I was able to pull up a template letter, complete it, have it verified by a member of my team, scan it, and email it to him—all within an hour of his call.

This client felt like he could contact me because I had let him know through my actions over the years that I meant it when I said that I was there to serve him. Each time I put my actions where my mouth is, I further cement that relationship. He won't forget that I was the advisor who was there to help him when he needed it.

LET THEM KNOW YOU
APPRECIATE THEIR BUSINESS

In his book *Elite Financial Teams: The 17% Solution*, Matt Oechsli talks about how to "surprise and delight" clients. They have a lot of choice when it comes to picking an advisor. As such, you want to make sure clients always know that you are honored and appreciative that they chose you. You can do this with words—nothing beats simply thanking someone—but you can also use events. I like to host client-appreciation events, which are limited to clients and their guests. I'll focus these events on things I know a particular group likes to do. I know what they like because I've listened to them and had real conversations, not just financial meetings. So, I might have a golf outing with four to six foursomes, a night at a show for music lovers, a clay shooting event, or a simple appreciation party at my house. The idea is to make sure the event is something they look forward to and shows that you really do know them as unique people. These events show appreciation, but they also put my clients at ease and give them an opportunity to develop a deeper personal relationship with me. I like to include my wife as often as possible in these events, and sometimes my children, as well. I am proud of my family and they make me look good. In addition, once your clients and their families get to *know* your family, they are more apt to open up about their personal and financial lives. This will allow you to become a better advisor in the long run, and allow your clients to know how much you appreciate their business.

BECOME A FOUNTAIN OF KNOWLEDGE

Clients will obviously look to you for investment advice, but if you want them to stay with you long term, as well as increase the assets you have under management, you need to build trust in a more holistic way. You want to provide that alpha level of service that sets you apart from other advisors. It's difficult but essential.

CONNECT WITH THE PROFESSIONALS
WHO ARE IMPORTANT TO THEM

Don't be afraid to call a client's CPA or tax attorney. Ask permission, but it is rare for clients to refuse to allow their professionals to interact. Call when they're not busy and say, "Hi. I just want to introduce myself. Joe Smith is a fairly new client. I know he gave you permission to speak with me. I just want to understand the tax situation of the family before I make any major transactions, so I can make them as tax efficient as possible." I want to make sure I educate myself effectively so that I can manage the portfolio in the best way possible. You know what happens with those phone calls? The CPA goes back to his client and says, "I heard from your advisor. He's the first one to ever call me and not ask for my business. He is only trying to do a good job for you." What client wouldn't love hearing that from one of their trusted professionals?

Advisors to the wealthy need to be a one-stop resource. If you do not sell insurance and your client needs an insurance agent, you want to be able to recommend not just anyone, but the best ones. If they need a real estate agent, you should have a good one you and/or your clients have a history with. Particularly in my practice, where I am often dealing with clients moving from a higher-tax state to Florida, I need to know who the best estate planners and tax attorneys are. You want to put your clients in front of other professionals who will make you look good, as well as refer clients back to you. I have a couple of tried-and-true methods to connect with the best professionals in my area.

Remember in the previous chapter, where I talked about setting up a network of professionals that meets once a month for breakfast? The idea behind this group isn't just to have others refer you to their clients (though that's a very good reason to do it), but rather to have a group of professionals you know and trust to recommend to your own clients. The more often you can provide a name to a client looking for one, the more likely that client will remember to refer you to their own friends when asked for an investment professional. I always give my clients two names—and usually one is a professional I have used myself.

One of the best ways to find the top professionals is to ask current clients whom they use. You are likely to hear the same two or three names over and over. Those are the ones you want to look into. Ask for a meeting and explain that your goal is to have another professional you can introduce to your clients. The question I want answered is, "Would I use this professional myself?" I will only recommend someone to my clients if the answer is yes.

My first priority is access. If a CPA and an attorney don't return my calls or emails in a timely manner, I won't use them. I want professionals to be at the top of their game, but not satisfied. I want them to be looking to grow their business, always current with new techniques and technology, and service oriented. In other words, I want them to have the same passion for serving and maintaining clients that I have. If they don't, I won't use them myself and won't refer them to clients.

Once you make a referral to your client, it is very important that you follow up to see how it went. These referrals are a reflection on you, and you want to make sure your clients are happy, and that the other professionals are as good as you think they are.

BECOME A SOLUTION PROVIDER
IN OTHER AREAS OF LIFE

It's also important to be active in the community. Professionals willing to serve as board members for local charities, schools, and companies are often the most successful in the community. Being involved with these professionals will expand an advisor's universe of names to recommend if a client is looking for a new CPA, real estate agent, primary doctor, or tutor for their child.

Advisors will also be more credible if they can say, "Here are a couple of names for you to check out. But this is who I use, and I've been really happy." I always put my money where my mouth is.

I was once hosting a golf event. I had hired a putting expert to do a little clinic before our tee times. After he was done, as we were getting ready to play the course, one of my clients walked up to me. I had met John back in 1999 when I was inviting CEOs of smaller healthcare companies to the conferences put on by Bear Stearns. More than ten years later, he ended up selling his company to a giant pharmaceutical firm and retiring to Florida. We had become good friends.

As we were walking to our carts, John stopped me and said, "You saved my life."

"What do you mean?" I asked, more than a little puzzled.

He then proceeded to tell me that he had been relying on my advice since he moved to the area. He had asked whom he should use for his real estate transactions, and I'd recommended an agent I knew and trusted. He had asked about a local attorney, and I gave him names of a couple of good ones. One of the questions he asked me was what primary care doctor he should use. I recommended my own doctor, whom I've grown to really trust. He has a closed practice, but I asked him to open it up for John and his wife, and he did.

When John went in for his physical, this doctor conducted a scan and found that John's carotid artery was 90 percent blocked, and he needed surgery right away. He could have had a stroke at any time. He had successful surgery two weeks later and is forever grateful that I referred him to this particular doctor.

Now, did I really save his life? Of course not! But because he knows I do extensive research on everyone I recommend, he trusted me. I believe John and his family will be my clients forever. I will really have to mess up for them to leave me—and I won't!

PROVIDE EDUCATION FOR CLIENTS, CHILDREN, AND SPOUSES

Wealthy clients aren't looking for an advisor who will simply put their assets into a standard portfolio and forget about it. They are looking for a partner in growing and protecting their wealth. One of the best ways to build a solid partnership with clients is to provide a variety of channels to educate them and their families. Every advisor has brochures and websites to recommend to their clients, but an elite advisor needs to do more.

PROVIDE ONE-ON-ONE INVESTING SESSIONS

Every client wants to believe that they are unique, so treat them that way. Set up meetings where you show them how to set up a trust that is beneficial to their particular situation. Show them specific techniques to help save taxes.

PROVIDE RESEARCH UPDATES THAT RELATE TO THEIR INVESTMENTS AND/OR INTERESTS

Clients want to know that you are monitoring their investments, and they want to know why you make the decisions you do. One of the best ways to keep clients on your side is to send them the research you are using. I will send them my firm's research but also updates from third-party firms. If your firm publishes research about healthcare, and you have clients in the healthcare field or in healthcare stocks, distribute that report to them with a quick email summary. If you have a report on what world events mean for their investments, distribute that. Education is both your and your clients' friend when it comes to successful investing. The more you can customize and give your clients what they are interested in, the more you can scale your business and create a service second to none. Assuming you and your firm do an adequate job managing their wealth, it is your service that will set you apart and spur your clients to give you unsolicited referrals.

PROVIDE NEXT GENERATION SUMMITS

"Shirtsleeves to shirtsleeves in three generations" isn't an urban myth. It's often how long it takes for wealth accumulated by one generation to be lost. To prevent that, clients want to know that their children will handle their inherited wealth wisely. I put together next-generation summits to make sure that happens.

Each of these summits is geared to the specific family I'm working with. I don't inundate the children with technical information. I don't confuse them. I first find out what their level of expertise is and what their life goals are. I then go from there. The summit can last from one to two days, and I'll often host it in New York so that I have access to experts from my firm who know how to communicate with the next generation. Since my team is so diverse, I will make sure to include team members of about the same age as the client's children. We'll start with simple things, such as credit and debit cards, and banking and lending. We'll talk about cybersecurity awareness and show them how easily their phones and computers can be hacked. And we'll show them the importance of making wise investment decisions, and how to do that. But we'll also have fun. We might go to a ball game if that's their interest. We might go to a show or on a historic tour. We'll make sure the day is focused on the kids and what they enjoy. At the end, they will know that I'm there to help them navigate the choices they'll have as they take control of the family wealth, but they'll also know that they now have the knowledge necessary to be a real partner in their own money management. These summits don't have to be expensive. It can be you sitting in the living room, at your office, or a hotel educating the next generation. But I have received so much traction with these events that I plan to do several per year.

SOME FINAL CONSIDERATIONS

Beyond the three main components of structural alpha, there are a couple of other issues to consider.

SEGMENT YOUR BUSINESS

If you really want to scale your business to grow it every year, you have to be very organized and efficient. This means that you will need to segment your business. As with most other aspects of my business, I try to keep this simple and clean. As much as I try to treat every client equally, not all relationships are treated in just the same way. I look at each client and determine the following:

- current revenues

- potential revenues

- center of influence

- time consumption

- total assets

I don't look at it as platinum, gold, and silver service, as many others do. All of our clients receive service over and above what is typically expected. However, we may reach out to our largest clients more frequently. Our largest clients will also have access to my cell phone. And the amount of time we spend on education may be more robust. Each advisor will have a method of segmenting clients, but the idea is to optimize your time, which is obviously limited.

WHEN TO FIRE A CLIENT

I hate to fire clients. However, it must be done at times. I remember speaking with a client who had significant assets with us. He would call weekly and seemed to always be in a bad mood, even if his portfolio was performing exceptionally well. He insisted things be done immediately and always had a special request. At the last two quarterly team meetings, my main assistant brought up his name as a chronic complainer and suggested we move on from him. Two weeks later, another team member was in tears after a phone call with him. That was it. I called the client and told him that he had to move his assets to someone else. He reminded me how much money he had with us. I told him that whenever he called, the collective blood pressure of our team rose, and there was no amount of money that would cure that. Unfortunately, this was a client that could never be satisfied. After our conversation, I remember a big sense of relief. My only regret is that I didn't do it sooner. Moral of the story: listen to your team and do not allow negative and impossible-to-please clients (no matter how much money they have) to ruin the camaraderie you are trying to create in your office.

BOTTOM LINE

Clients tend to leave their advisors for two reasons:

1. They feel taken for granted because the advisors do not communicate with them. I have had many clients tell me they are leaving their other advisor because they do not hear from them often enough.

2. They do not understand your investment philosophy.

Investment performance is certainly important, but I will never tell my clients that it's my job to outperform the market (though I am very proud of our investment performance). Instead, I want to give them a bear hug. I want to be so intertwined with my clients that they think, *Investment performance is one of the top ten reasons I trust Sal and his team, but not the number one reason.*

The number one reason is that I surround my clients with structural alpha, providing them with service over and above anything they would ever expect. My clients don't leave, because they know I care, and my clients are my number one focus.

Now on to that second point—investment philosophy. I want to be my clients' CFO, and they all know exactly why they own the investments we put them in. I'll explain my philosophy—and suggest how you can develop your own—in the next chapter.

KEY TAKEAWAYS

- Clients don't care how much you know until they know how much you care.

- Make yourself and your team irreplaceable.

- Surround your clients with Four Seasons-like service and Amazon-like efficiency.

- Segment your client base.

- Don't let one difficult client ruin the camaraderie of your team.

- Focus on the long-term client, not on your short-term pocketbook.

CHAPTER 6
YOUR WEALTH MANAGEMENT STRATEGY

HOW OFTEN DO YOU approach prospect meetings by touting your investment performance? It's understandable. We are, after all, investment advisors, so claiming to regularly beat the benchmarks seems a natural way to sell services. But if you sell performance, you sell failure—it's so difficult to outperform the market nowadays that promising to always do so is a recipe for disappointment. And disappointing clients is a sure way to lose them.

That being said, you are a financial advisor. Investment performance is important. As a successful advisor, you don't always have to outperform, but you cannot consistently underperform. Clients who consistently experience subpar investment performance will leave. They will also leave if they do not understand your investment philosophy or you cannot articulate it effectively. So, how do you keep clients happy since it is impossible to guarantee consistent outperformance?

Wrap your clients in structural alpha as discussed in the previous chapter.

- Have a simple investment philosophy.

- Be able to communicate that philosophy.

- Execute it consistently and systematically.

- Provide educational resources for your clients so they can act as true partners in their own financial decisions.

- Always make sure your clients know you are acting in their best interests.

HAVE A SIMPLE INVESTMENT PHILOSOPHY

Some investment advisors make investment philosophies and strategies more complicated than they need to be. There are really only three general buckets of investment strategies. Which an advisor chooses to use in their practice is dependent on their personal comfort with each one, as well as the comfort of their clients. The most important thing is to have an overall basic philosophy, articulate it to your clients, and then customize to the family's risk-return profile.

PASSIVE ASSET MANAGEMENT

This usually involves tracking an index to guarantee that returns match those of the overall market. When put into practice, it's less expensive than other investment strategies and is easy for the client to understand. It's a great way to invest when markets are going up. It's more problematic when they are going down.

ACTIVE ASSET MANAGEMENT

This type of management involves moving in and out of markets and sectors as the economy and trends change. The goal is to outperform the blended benchmark that is set up front. This strategy often is more expensive than passive strategies because it involves more research, manager time, and/or commissions on buying and selling assets. An exceptional manager can often generate alpha-level returns with this strategy, but clients also have to be ready to ride out volatility if the markets are choppy and the manager is having a difficult time finding opportunities.

TACTICAL ASSET MANAGEMENT

This style relies on timing (often with algorithms) and triggers to move in and out of various positions to protect assets. Advisors who use this model will move assets from equities to bonds or cash if a market falls by a certain percentage and reverse the flow if the market is rising. It is considered a good way to prevent large losses, but investors can find their capital parked in bonds and cash for long periods of time if the right trigger points are not reached, thus limiting returns.

Choosing one of these broad strategies isn't an either/or situation. I like to combine aspects of each of the three broad strategies into a hybrid strategy that has served me well. In addition to choosing a general way to execute investments, I've found several ancillary factors that have helped keep my investments focused on what is best for my clients and have contributed to excellent performance over the years.

INVEST IN WHAT YOU KNOW

One of the major influences on my investment philosophy was Peter Lynch's book *One Up on Wall Street.* At the time the book came out in 1989, Lynch was enjoying an unprecedented run as the portfolio manager of the Fidelity Magellan Fund. It can be credibly argued that he was personally responsible for opening equities investment to the everyday investor, as he proved that reliable returns could be achieved in the mutual fund format.

In his book, Lynch explains how to use what you already know to make money in the market. That really resonated with me, and I bought into Lynch's school of thought: buy what you know and use, as long as you trust the management and balance sheets of the companies.[11]

In 1993, when my oldest son was just a month old, my wife asked if we owned Procter & Gamble stock. She had never expressed an interest in our stock portfolio before—she knows that's what I do for a living, and her interests lie elsewhere—so I wondered where this came from.

"Why do you ask?"

"Everything I buy for this baby is made by Procter & Gamble," she explained. "Diapers, wipes, creams—you name it." Add in paper goods, detergents, and soaps, and we had P&G products in nearly every room in the house.

The next day, I analyzed its balance sheet, liked what I saw, and personally bought one hundred shares at approximately $100/share. A few days later it split three for one. Over time, I added to my stake. I thought, "If I'm going to spend all this money on the baby, maybe one day the dividends will help me cover the expenses."

As I looked around further, I realized it wasn't just P&G products that we used all the time. When I got up every morning, I used Gillette razor blades and shaving cream. I used Gillette's Right Guard for deodorant, and I brushed my teeth with an Oral B toothbrush. God knows how many Duracell (owned by Gillette at the time) batteries I bought. I did my due diligence on the company, again liked what I saw, and started buying Gillette. (And it didn't hurt that it was a local, Boston-based company.) The same thought

---

11   Lynch, with Rothchild, *One Up On Wall Street: How To Use What You Already Know To Make Money In The Market*, 2nd ed.

process occurred: perhaps I could earn enough from dividends and growth of the common stock to pay for all of my products.

Over the years, Procter & Gamble and Gillette became two of my biggest positions. And they proved themselves to be stable, reliable investments time after time. Then, in January of 2005, it was announced that Procter & Gamble was acquiring Gillette in a $57 billion deal, its largest acquisition ever at the time.[12] There is not a better feeling than seeing a company you own featured on the front page of the *Wall Street Journal* in a takeout!

KEEP IT SIMPLE

As mentioned before, one of the main reasons clients leave advisors is that they don't understand what the advisor is doing with their money. And the reason they don't understand is that many advisors don't have a simple, consistent strategy. They put clients into their firm's products without a thought as to how those products might conflict or overlap. Having a simple, consistent investment philosophy that everyone on the team can articulate in less than thirty seconds, one that is easily communicated to clients, will go a long way to engendering trust and keeping your clients on your side as active partners.

INVEST FOR THE LONG HAUL AND AVOID FADS

Advisors need to act as trusted fiduciaries for their clients. On a practical, actionable level, this often translates to "buy and hold" or "avoid moving in and out of fads or trendy stock." It doesn't mean that you can't make money with trading strategies—a lot of people do—but a lot of people also lose their shirts, and this isn't the advisor's money to lose. When I encounter clients looking to take

---

12   Vries, "Procter & Gamble Acquires Gillette."

on additional risk in equities, I will typically place their assets in a core strategy and be tactical around the perimeter of that strategy. I will also bring on additional experts who specialize in the particular asset class, such as small-mid cap, international, or alternatives. When it comes to higher-risk alternative strategies, I will only suggest third-party managers who have been approved by my firm. Why? Because I don't want my clients wandering into another Bernie Madoff situation. If my firm has done the due diligence and backs the strategy, I am confident the clients will be taken care of if an investment ever becomes part of a fraud investigation.

I have always shied away from investing in fads, especially industries or companies that have absurd valuations that I can't rationalize. There have been a lot of them over my career. Many years ago, Mexican stocks first made their debut as American Depository Receipts (ADRs) on the NYSE. Soon, it seemed every Mexican company went public, and investors began buying anything based in Mexico, without regard to what the company did or its valuation. The same behavior was seen decades ago with the biotech sector. More recently, Bitcoin was something everyone had to own.

Is Bitcoin a fad or a real thing? I don't know. But until I can understand it and explain it clearly to my clients, I can't recommend it. Warren Buffett has been quoted as saying, "Never invest in a business you cannot understand," and I have embraced that sentiment. The bottom line is, if your unsophisticated relatives are telling everyone at the Thanksgiving table about how much money they are making in the stock market on the new craze, it is a fad and time to get out.

Instead, I keep it simple. I invest in the tried-and-true companies I know—companies with a long track record of posting dividends and growth numbers. In general, I like dividend aristocrat stocks because I can count on them. These are large cap stocks—usually $10 billion or more—on the S&P 500 Index that have increased their dividends for at least twenty-five consecutive years. Past performance might not be a *guarantee* of future performance, but it is undoubtedly a very strong indicator.

BET ON THE JOCKEY

When it comes to choosing an investment opportunity, I like to bet on the jockey rather than the horse. This could be the portfolio manager at an investment firm, the management of a publicly traded company, or the entrepreneur at a new venture. The actual company doesn't matter as much as the team governing it. The companies with the best management historically outperform those not as well managed.

Betting on management and people is also a philosophy I embrace in my personal life. In the early 2000s, I was coaching youth hockey. One day, another coach called me and said, "Sal, I got your number from a mutual friend who thought you might be interested in a business opportunity that I'm working on. Can I stop by tomorrow and talk to you?" I only knew him as a hockey dad and coach, but he had a reputation as a good guy, so I agreed to hear him out.

During our meeting, he explained that the local mom-and-pop retail store, where we bought all our kids' hockey, baseball, and football gear, was for sale. He had a background in retail and wanted to buy it and turn it into a focused hockey outlet. But he needed financing. His plan was to find three outside investors to join him in the venture. He had the numbers to back him up. He also had the passion and drive to succeed as an entrepreneur. He told me that when the store grew to $5 million in revenues, he would leave his current company and be the CEO.

I had admired how he dealt with the kids on the ice, and I knew he was a really good person. Now he was showing me his business side, and I was impressed.

I looked at him and I said, "Why do we need two more partners?"

He said, "Quite frankly, I can't come up with the entire amount, so I figured I'd get three others to help out."

I said, "You put in what you can, and I'll take care of the rest. I'll give you an interest-free loan. You pay me back whenever you can."

He looked at me and said, "You would do that?"

I said, "If this thing works, it is going to be you who makes it happen. And if we are going to be partners, we have to trust each other. I'm putting my best foot forward with trust. I just need your guarantee that you are the one who will run this once it gets to $5 million. I'm betting on you personally." He paid back the loan within a year.

We purchased that one general sporting goods store in 2002 with six employees. Today, Pure Hockey has grown well into nine figures in revenues, has fifty-four locations in eighteen states with more than one thousand employees, and is the largest specialty hockey retailer in the country—and it's still growing. My son, who was an eight-year-old hockey player when we started the venture, worked at corporate headquarters outside of Boston for several years. My partner, David Nectow, is like a brother to me. There is no way this specialty retailer would be so successful if I hadn't bet on him. Investing in a retailer was the last thing on my mind when my partner approached me in 2002. But I bet on him!

In any elite practice, many of the clients are likely entrepreneurs, and they represent a perfect example of betting on the jockey. Their situations are different from those of corporate executives, who come in with restricted stock, a pension plan, bonuses, and other compensation incentives. Entrepreneurs have very different needs.

I always tell my entrepreneurial clients that the best investment they can make is in themselves. I will never pretend to compete with the returns they can make investing in their own company.

I tell them that when they want to retire or simply need to take some chips off the table to be a bit more conservative, they can come to me, and I'll take care of the rest. I let them know that my job is not to compete with what they can do by investing in themselves, but to protect and preserve the assets they have accumulated over the years and to give them a decent rate of return without undue risk. They love to hear that.

BE CONSISTENT

Once you have an investment philosophy, you need to execute it consistently. Don't change stripes in the middle of the game. For example, if you are a value investor, don't try to be a growth investor just because it's become the strategy of the day. It won't work.

In the same vein, I've found that using a buy-and-hold strategy has resulted in better performance than trying to time the market. That doesn't mean that you should never tweak your investments. Of course you should—when it is warranted. But you don't want to jump in and out of positions on a whim. I like to buy well-managed companies for the long-term. But even great companies can temporarily have absurd valuations at times. I prefer to reduce exposure (but not necessarily liquidate completely) when the valuation is historically inflated and to add to an existing position when its valuation is lower than normal. This "contrarian" style has served our clients well. Warren Buffett once said all there is to investing is picking good stocks at good times and sticking with them, as long as they remain good stocks. That philosophy has worked for him, and it has worked for me, as well.

EXECUTING YOUR PHILOSOPHY

Once you have settled on a simple, consistent philosophy, you need to find a model that allows you to execute with consistency. There are a lot of good investment models out there.

USE YOUR FIRM'S MODELS

Most firms have their own investment portfolios. These will include models covering a variety of strategies, as well as risk and return profiles. Advisors can mix and match to find the right ones for their clients.

This is the approach many advisors take when they are starting out. These portfolios are managed by professionals and take the guesswork out of which equity or fund to buy. However, a conscientious advisor will look at the specific components of a portfolio. There is often overlap in the equities and industries represented in various portfolios, even if the overall risk profiles are different. If you put your client in several portfolios to diversify their assets, you could end up unintentionally overweighting a company that might be in several portfolios or actually increasing risk with too much concentration in a single industry. Be aware of the portfolio composition so you can choose wisely.

USE THIRD-PARTY MANAGERS (SEPARATELY MANAGED ACCOUNTS OR MUTUAL FUNDS)

Most major firms have an internal research team that offers a variety of third-party, separately managed accounts (SMAs) on their platform. There are thousands of money managers and hundreds of strategies. The research team will have vetted and analyzed them all and have found those that have offered consistent, reliable performance at a reasonable fee over several years. These are then added to the firm's approved-manager list. This list will include several large-, medium-, and small-cap managers, as well as emerging market managers, fixed-income managers, alternative investment managers, global managers, etc. Using this list means you don't have to do due diligence on every manager—it's been done for you by professionals—and you can save money on fees because a money manager will typically reduce its fees to be on your bank's or financial services firm's approved list. It is still up to the advisor, however, to choose those managers who work best for their own strategy. If you decide to use this approach, make sure you get to know the third-party managers very well and use them when you do future events. They all have marketing budgets and will be more than willing to help educate you and your clients about their products. And they will pay for it.

If you want to use this approach, my suggestion is to be very knowledgeable about the firm's entire approved list but keep the number of managers you actually work with small—only use two or three in each asset class. It is best to keep the choices narrow and deep. I emphasized this strategy for quite a number of years.

BUILD YOUR OWN PORTFOLIOS

As their practice grows, many advisors typically hire their own chief investment officers and manage their own model portfolios. They usually continue to rely on their parent firm's approved list for some strategies, but managing a few of their own portfolios allows them to buy and sell equities when they see opportunities, as well as manage portfolios that truly represent their investment philosophy. The downside of this approach is that advisors are also responsible for any underperformance. If they were using third-party managers from an approved list, they could swap one manager out for another if it is underperforming. If they are managing the portfolio, however, they don't have that option.

COMBINE THE BEST OF SEVERAL STRATEGIES

This is what I do. I use both my firm's approved list and my own portfolios. We typically manage all of the large cap investments inside our team, but we use select third-party managers for specialty asset classes, such as small cap, international, and alternatives.

Pulling out the best features of several strategies is one way to differentiate yourself. I like to use my own portfolio models, but I can add funds or special situation strategies from my parent firm if they are prudent for a particular client. I can suggest that a client invest in one of my model portfolios, while doing a couple of tactical trades to make the investment strategy work for the client. Being able to tweak a client's portfolio, rather than rely solely on my firm's models, differentiates my practice and gives my clients extra value on the investment side.

Which strategy you choose will depend on your firm's offerings and capabilities—if you are new to the business or in a small office, you might not be able to manage your own portfolios—but your choice also has a lot to do with what you are comfortable with.

MAKE IT SCALABLE

No matter which model you choose, you want to make sure it is scalable. You are never going to be able to have fifty clients with fifty unique portfolios, each containing twenty-five or more different equity positions. That would be impossible to manage. Instead, you want to have just a few model portfolios that are suitable for the vast majority of your clients, while still maintaining some customization for each family. This isn't as difficult as you might think.

Broadly speaking, there are only four risk-return profiles: speculative, growth, moderate, and conservative. Models to support these profiles range from speculative portfolios that emphasize almost all equities to conservative portfolios that favor fixed income. Knowing that your clients will almost surely fit in one of these four buckets means that you only need to manage the number of portfolios that match your philosophy and comfort zone. For example, I'm not the right advisor for someone who wants to speculate by day trading, so I don't have a speculative portfolio. I do, however, manage growth, moderate, and conservative portfolios. My clients typically fit into one of these buckets, with very few exceptions. That means all of my growth clients have similar portfolios, all of my moderate clients have similar portfolios, and all of my conservative clients have similar portfolios. If my chief investment officer decides to make a change in my model growth portfolio, he will make the same change for every growth client at the same time at the same price.

If your model portfolios fit the majority of your clients' needs, you will have the time and ability to customize a client's portfolio when warranted. For example, if a client is the CEO of a major pharmaceutical company, much of the client's net worth is probably already dependent on the market's view of that industry sector. If my model growth portfolio contains a large-cap pharmaceutical stock, I will replace it with a company in a different sector. After all, my client already has enough of this sector through his own company.

DO THE RIGHT THING FOR YOUR CLIENTS

I tell my clients that I eat my own cooking. I won't recommend anything that I wouldn't invest in myself if I had the same investment profile. And you should be investing yourself. It is important to have your own financial plan, whether you are a rookie or a twenty-five-year veteran. If you have been in the industry for twenty years and you don't have any of your own assets in the markets (equities, fixed income, alternatives), then how can you possibly expect to create these plans, monitor them, and manage your clients' expectations? My clients know I have been investing in the markets alongside of them since I was twenty-five years old. So, when their portfolios go down, mine does, as well. It's more credible to tell them to hang on if I can tell them I'm hanging on, too.

I was having lunch with a client early one summer. At that time, most of the dividend aristocrat stocks, which are investments I favor, were down. These are mostly recession-resistant companies that have paid dividends quarter after quarter for more than twenty-five years. Yet, here I sat, looking at a client who was asking why they were down, many by double digits, when the overall market was still setting records.

So, I rattled off a number of the bigger names and noted how far they were off their highs in the first half. I looked at the client and said, "You own them all." Before she could react, I added, "I also own them all." I then pointed out that despite the drop of some of the big blue chip stocks, her overall portfolio was still positive because she also owned some big name stocks that were recording personal bests.

I went further and told her that I was not worried about any of the dividend aristocrat companies. We'd owned them for a long time, and they kept increasing their dividends. They would rebound over the long term.

Clients appreciate it when you tell them that you own the same stocks they do. They love to know that you are alongside them and have the same skin in the game.

Putting your clients first really underlies everything else you do as an advisor. If you treat them like family, do the right thing, and invest for them the way you would for yourself, it's very likely that you'll end up with clients who will be with you for generations.

KEY TAKEAWAYS

- Don't compete on investment performance alone.

- Place your bets on stability—not fads.

- Keep it simple and consistent.

- Do the right thing for your clients.

- Make your investment models scalable.

CHAPTER 7

YOU CAN'T DO IT ALONE: BUILDING AND MANAGING A TEAM

IN MARCH OF 2008, Bear Stearns was acquired by J.P. Morgan. That meant I had a choice to make: go to a competitor, start my own company, or stay with J.P. Morgan. After a few weeks of thought, I decided that J.P. Morgan gave me a tremendous opportunity to expand the product offerings to my clients. I could now offer banking products, such as savings, credit cards, and debit cards, as well as lending and credit opportunities, such as mortgages. I was also interested in being part of the firm's future growth plans. At the time, JPMorgan Chase & Co. only had nine branches in Florida.[13] However, it was in the process of acquiring 2,239 Washington Mutual retail offices from the FDIC. Approximately two hundred of those branches, which were soon to be rebranded as JPMorgan Chase outlets, were in Florida.[14] In addition to converting the Washington Mutual branches, the firm had plans to open its own branches over the next few years. Today, JPMorgan Chase has more than four hundred branches in the state, doubling its presence in just ten years, and it expects to grow by about 10 percent in the next three years.[15]

---

13 Mann Jr., "Gateway City/Who's Here: Chase a major player in Florida banking since 2009."

14 Letzing, "WaMu seized, sold to J.P. Morgan Chase."

15 Florida Trend, "JPMorgan Chase to Add 35 Branches in Florida in Next Three Years."

JPMorgan Chase was the only bank in the country expanding during the worst recession since the Great Depression, and it was doing so right in my backyard of South Florida. The opportunity to be part of this growth story was too good to pass up. I also knew that investors were extremely sensitive about the health of the banking industry—they were seeing major financial institutions dissolve before their eyes—and being at one of the most powerful and safest banks in the world would help alleviate my clients' concerns.

With the ability to add so many new banking services, I needed to hire someone who understood each of these products and how they could help my clients. But first I had to convince the firm to let me hire when everyone else was reducing head count. I have a good relationship with my firm, so when I told my manager, Rick Penafiel, what I wanted—and offered to split the cost with him—he agreed it was a good idea.

The next hurdle was to find someone familiar with the products I would soon be offering my clients. Because they were JPMorgan Chase products, it made sense to look in a Chase branch.

So, I walked into a Chase branch near my office and approached a woman at the information desk in the lobby. "I need help with my personal finances, including a potential line of credit and mortgage. Which one of your bankers is the best?"

She said, "They're all very good. I can't recommend one over the other."

In a whisper, I told her, "I just want to make sure I'm working with the best. It's a very complicated situation. And I really don't want to stay with Bank of America next door."

She looked around, then quietly responded, also in a whisper, "Daniel is the best."

Daniel was busy, so I asked for his business card and left. A week later, I walked into the same branch, asked a teller the same question, and she gave me the same answer.

I went back to my office and called Daniel, leaving a message that I'd like to talk to him about an opportunity. We met several times over the next few months, and his manager was very supportive of him pursuing a new challenge.

I hired Daniel initially because he was very familiar with the Chase product offerings and was a personal banker. At first, he was our credit and lending expert. Eventually, with my blessing and encouragement, Daniel took the courses necessary for higher-level licenses and certifications. He now holds CFA, CFP, CWPA, and CIMA designations. Daniel became my right-hand man and was instrumental in helping solve our clients' problems from the moment I hired him; he has been irreplaceable in growing our business. He has earned the respect of our team, the firm, and more importantly, our clients.

The acquisition of Bear Stearns by J.P. Morgan was the impetus for me to reach out and expand my in-house dedicated team. For most advisors, the timing isn't as clear-cut. But at some point, advisors who want to build an elite practice are going to have to build a personal internal team that can offer the services their clients want. Wealthy clients want a one-stop shop, and very few advisors are able to do it all themselves. In fact, I don't know any elite advisor who hasn't pulled together a team of highly qualified professionals.

Advisors often hire someone who can complement their own skills (i.e., someone who is strong where they are weak) and, thus, allow the company to offer additional services. Others look for a mini-me to double down on the strengths that set the practice apart. Still, others look for the brightest people—those they just have to have—and then create roles for them. In my case, I always identified a need and then found the right person to fill that role. But no matter which strategy you decide works best for your specific situation—and often it really is just how you personally want to work—I think teams work best if you start with two specific hires.

THAT FIRST HIRE—
A TRUSTED ASSISTANT OR CLIENT ASSOCIATE

The person you hire first can set the tone for the rest of the team, so you want to give it some real thought.

Normally, the first hire will be a shared sales assistant or client associate. These are the people who keep your practice running smoothly, leaving you free to focus on revenue-producing activities. They answer the phone, handle the documentation, and are the first line of defense in servicing the needs of the clients. As you grow your business, this person will become the practice manager.

Looking for a shared client associate, rather than someone dedicated solely to your practice, has two advantages. You can usually turn to your firm to provide someone who is already experienced in the industry and, thus, needs little training. This person will typically already be working for other advisors and will know exactly what you need. Your firm will often cover at least half of the salary, and sometimes the entire salary, making this first hire extremely affordable.

If you do not want to use a shared assistant, or your firm doesn't provide one, you may, like many advisors, start out with a part-time assistant and then add hours and/or days as your practice grows.

Eventually, you will be doing enough business to justify having your own practice manager. If you hire right, this person will become an integral part of the business.

My practice manager keeps my calendar, organizes and runs the team meetings, and is responsible for gauging revenue and profitability goals. She helps segment clients, and deals with the internal workings of the firm, including compliance, marketing, and management. Overall, she keeps me away from the time-draining things necessary to manage a practice or business. She knows my time is best spent directly with clients, either in person or on the phone. Any activity not directly related to that is delegated to her—and in many instances, she will delegate it from there.

As a business grows, the number of non-revenue-producing issues also grow. Organized, skilled practice managers are worth their weight in gold if they can take care of these issues and keep the business running smoothly, leaving you free to focus on prospects and clients. My first assistant was with me for twenty-seven years. I can honestly say my business wouldn't be what it is today without her help.

This hire needs to be someone who is capable of being the go-to person. This is not just a paper pusher. This employee is often the first contact a prospect or client has with the office, so you want someone who projects the same attitude and customer-first service that you would if you were answering the phone yourself. He/she should be able to understand and articulate how accounts are handled and solve routine problems on their own. You are going to want to let your assistant or client associate get involved in really running the business, so you can be the rainmaker and advisor.

In my case, I looked for someone intelligent, organized, unflappable, and sociable. But more than that, I wanted someone with whom I really clicked. This was going to be the person I spent the majority of my day with and relied on to treat my clients the way I would treat them.

I screen for fit by spending most of the interview talking about things other than business skills. I've found that a person's family interactions will give me a good idea of whether we have a good fit. The bottom line is that you want to be able to trust your assistant to give your clients the same level of more-than-expected service that you have built your practice on.

THE SECOND HIRE—RAINMAKING HELP

The second hire is typically somebody who is going to help source business, because if you are not growing your business, your business is dying.

This person could be someone just starting out that you'd like to train and help get established, or it could be an experienced pro. The person, however experienced, needs to be driven, motivated, organized, energetic, and have a great work ethic, as well as a thick skin. (See chapter 4 for more details.)

Back when I was relatively new in the business, I recognized the need to have someone help me prospect so that I could focus on closing and on building relationships with existing clients. At that time, prospecting generally consisted of cold calling, and it was more productive for me to focus on warmer prospects.

Today, we make fewer cold calls, but we still need to build our pipeline. Putting distribution lists together for targeted mailings and emails containing appropriate research and other information that we provide for clients on a consistent basis could be part of this hire's duties. This person should always be prospecting and thinking of ways to bring in new clients!

ADDING ON FROM THERE

After you have someone onboard to handle the administrative part of the business, as well as someone who can help bring in new business, additional personnel will depend on the size and focus of your practice or company. Over time, I've hired someone to do all the financial planning and someone else to do the estate planning. I decided that I wanted to manage the investments in-house, so I hired a chief investment officer to do the research and analysis. I've hired a classic marketer to oversee our social media outreach, as well as write and design brochures, reports, and presentations and raise the profile of our practice in the community and the industry. Other practices might have professionals who specialize in insurance, fixed-income strategies, or alternative asset classes.

Many of these additional hires can be brought in on a freelance or contract basis in the beginning. If the parent firm allows it, interns can provide additional help during busy times. In addition, advisors can use professionals from their networking group or virtual team until their practice has reached the size to justify expenditures for full-time professionals.

HOW TO FIND GOOD PEOPLE

Sourcing good people is crucial to the success of a team. My methods of finding the right people for my team are similar to my prospecting activities.

UTILIZE THE RESOURCES OF YOUR FIRM

One of the ways to inexpensively add services to a practice is to use the resources of the firm that you work for. A lot of firms have insurance specialists, financial planning experts, estate planning experts, fixed-income experts, derivatives experts, and others who can provide services to clients. These experts are usually housed wherever the firm is headquartered, but a number of the larger firms have regional offices, as well, so they might be closer than you think.

Using these specialists is like having a virtual team you can call on whenever you need them, but you don't have to pay them out of your own pocket. Some advisors find that using their firm's resources is all they need to grow their business, but most advisors reach a point where they want at least a couple of specialists on their own team. Earlier in my career, I worked exclusively with those specialists that my firm provided. Today, I still use many of them, but, as my business matured, I felt it was more powerful to have experts who compliment the firm's resources on my own team.

RELY ON THOSE YOU KNOW

One of the benefits of working for J.P. Morgan is the many business bankers in the area. Several years ago, Daniel and I always seemed to find ourselves in front of one particular banker who was very driven to grow his business. We first met him soon after he had been assigned as the local banker for our area, when he picked up the phone to introduce himself. During the following two years, we were impressed with how he conducted himself, how organized he was, and how he seemed to know instinctively which clients to refer to us because we would be a good fit. We also referred business to him. For example, if we had a client who needed a business banking relationship, we would refer that client to Jason. And all of our clients came back raving about how professional and helpful he was.

More importantly, his clients respected him, and he had high ethical standards. Over time a friendship developed, and I thought he would make a great team member. So, I made him an offer to manage the marketing and become a rainmaker on our team. He is now in charge of our marketing full time. He knows how to speak the business banker language, so many of his former colleagues trust him with their clients' wealth management needs. From organizing the pipeline to managing our events, Jason is simply the most organized banker I know and a great team member.

This hire has worked so well because we knew Jason's personality, work ethic, and skill set; we knew he'd fit into our culture. Basically, we had already had a two-year job interview. In addition, he had the connections we were looking for to help grow the business. When he came onboard, his focus was to deepen our bonds with the community of centers of influences. This came naturally to him since it was exactly what he was doing in his prior banking position. Thus, he connects with bankers, CPAs, and attorneys to let them know what we can do for their clients. These are the people who will refer business to us, the same way we refer to them. Jason makes sure that I always have people on my calendar who can source business to us.

Another example is also someone I already knew through a working relationship. He managed the municipal bond department at J.P. Morgan, and before that he managed the Bear Stearns municipal department. Because so many of my clients are high-net-worth individuals, I have spoken with him an average of five times per day for the past twenty years. Over the years, he became one of my best friends at the firm. I trusted him implicitly and knew his intentions were always to do the right thing for the client. He was reaching retirement age but wasn't ready to retire. He was ready, however, to try something new. We talked about how he could help my team, and he jumped at the chance. He now heads our team's fixed-income efforts.

More recently in my career, I decided to pool resources with two long time successful advisors, Louise and John. This was a mutual decision between the three of us to become partners. Louise and I were colleagues at the same firm my entire career, but I got to know her better over the past ten years. She always had a stellar reputation at the firm, but I found out firsthand that she is one of the most knowledgeable and hardworking advisors I've ever encountered. We worked jointly on a few clients together, and became close friends. Over time it was only natural to form a more formal partnership. Similarly, John had moved from San Francisco to Palm Beach and sat in the office next to me. Over the course of a couple of years, I was very impressed with his knowledge of the markets and the care with which he handled his clients. It wasn't long before I started to seek his opinions on the various investment products he was utilizing for his clients. Today, I am proud to call Louise and John partners and close friends. In each case, I had been able to witness their business ethics and the care they took handling their clients long before we decided to join forces.

Looking at professionals you already work with takes most of the risk out of a new hire. You know how they interact with clients or colleagues. You know their work ethic. You know their skills. You aren't relying on a third-party reference who may or may not put the same emphasis on client service that you do. You are, instead, partnering with a known quantity.

RELY ON RECOMMENDATIONS FROM TRUSTED PROFESSIONALS

In my story about hiring Daniel, I knew I needed someone with banking, credit, and customer service experience. Where better to find someone like that than in a bank? And what better bank than one in my own network? I didn't know anyone at that particular branch, but I felt confident that anyone working there would have the minimum qualifications I was looking for, given their high standards. Then, by asking for the best, I was able to identify Daniel. When looking for in-house experts, reach out to those in your network whom you respect and trust. Ask whom they use for their insurance, estate planning, banking, and other professional services. This strategy should give you a handful of highly qualified, well-respected prospects to approach.

RELY ON GROUPS AND ASSOCIATIONS YOU ARE AFFILIATED WITH

I've found that groups and associations that share my values are a good place to look for team members. For example, we have openings for an intern each year. I'm a member of the local Dartmouth alumni association and am also a board member at a local private high school. I have found that the interns sourced through these groups have almost always worked out. We want to hire interns who can add value, and working through the professional and alumni groups that I'm part of has worked well in finding what we need.

DON'T RUSH IT

I don't normally advertise open positions—I prefer to find someone through my network—but when it came time to hire an analyst who would, I hoped, become my chief investment officer, I thought I should cast a wider net. So, I asked my firm to advertise the position. We received more than 75 applications. A colleague at headquarters sorted through them and sent me the ones they thought best met my requirements. I read through the résumés and ended up interviewing ten applicants. From there, I narrowed it down to two finalists, whom I met with a second time. They were both young, hungry, and very good at their job.

At this point in the hiring process, I brought my team in to meet with each finalist. I have always maintained that before we hire anyone, the entire team needs to be unanimous in the belief that the position is needed. Then, they all need to agree on the person we hire.

After meeting with both candidates, my team was ready to hire one of them. But I wasn't. On a scale of one to ten, he was just at a six or a seven. And that wasn't good enough. My team agreed that the best candidate was only about the middle of the scale, but he was the best we had.

Instead of hiring someone we weren't 100 percent happy with, we decided to ask our internal recruiter to send more résumés. One of the new résumés jumped out, because I knew where the applicant lived. It was obvious he had grown up in an environment that would make it easy for him to interact with our clients without being intimidated by their wealth. That was a good start. But I needed to know if he had the right work ethic. I called him in, and we began to talk. I found out that he had been a baseball player at Wake Forest, now worked for a hedge fund, and had a very close family. The fact that he had been a college baseball player made me think he was a hard worker, but I wanted to know how important this job was to him, and how persistent he was. So, when he called a few days later, I didn't return his call on purpose. A couple of weeks went by, and I got an email from him asking where we were in the process and reiterating his interest. So, we met again, and I again didn't call him. This went on for a couple of months until I was convinced he was persistent enough for the job. Greg has turned out to be exactly what I hoped for and is now my trusted chief investment officer.

I don't think the outcome would have been nearly as successful if we had hired the first candidate. Taking your time when you are hiring is critical.

WHAT TO LOOK FOR

When expanding your team, the key is knowing what characteristics you want to have in your new hire. No matter what position I am hiring for—whether it is an intern or a chief investment officer—there are a few qualities I've found to be most important.

INTELLIGENCE

There are many varieties of intelligence, but I want someone well-read, curious, and able to pick up nuances. If someone is interested in learning, I can teach the person everything else. I also look for team members with a high emotional quotient (EQ). EQ and common sense are valued more highly on my team than IQ points!

PROFESSIONALISM

This quality is difficult to explain, but you know professionalism when you see it. In general, it means being honest, reliable, confident, and poised. It means providing outstanding service 100 percent of the time. Most of all, it means being ethical. This industry has gotten a black eye recently because of a lack of ethics in both rank-and-file members and high-profile practitioners. It is up to everyone who loves this business to change that perception by acting in the best interests of the client at all times.

TECHNOLOGICAL SOUNDNESS

The technology and software available to advisors and clients are improving and expanding at an exponential rate. I don't believe that artificial intelligence software or programmatic investment platforms will replace advisors in wealth management, but we need to know how to use those platforms to provide top-level service. Clients like being able to access and monitor their investments and accounts online. This is an additional way to offer structural alpha service. In our office, Daniel is our technology guru. He actually used to work at Best Buy in college. As part of our above-and-beyond service, he has even gone to clients' houses and set up their online bill pay accounts, as well as their investment profile and access.

CLIENT FOCUS

Too often analysts and advisors get wrapped up in the numbers and beating the benchmark, and they forget that the business is all about people. I have set my business apart from others by becoming more than just an investment advisor. I've become a key component in my clients' lives. Everyone on my team jumps to help clients in any way they can, whether it is analyzing an investment or suggesting a great new restaurant.

SOCIAL SKILLS

Social skills are often considered a soft skill, but being able to confidently interact with prospects, clients, and centers of influence is crucial to providing service to clients. Every member of my team can answer a phone, greet a client walking in the door, or mingle at events and make everyone they interact with feel at ease. All are able to carry on interesting conversations, and those chats are rarely all about investment accounts. We want our clients to look forward to talking and interacting with us.

INTEREST IN HELPING OTHERS

Financial advising is a service industry. Unfortunately, those looking to make a living in the industry are not always interested in helping others. This business can, indeed, be very lucrative. But I don't want team members who are in it just for the money. I want people who will go the extra mile, spend the extra time, and put in the extra effort to provide our clients with service over and above anything they would ever expect. And I want them to do it because they get pleasure from providing that level of service. I want good people.

ABILITY TO RELATE TO CLIENTS

It is important to have a team that reflects your clients. This means you want a diverse team with varied skills, backgrounds, ages, etc. Team members need to have some things in common, so they will mesh into a cohesive unit—similar values, work ethics, client focus—but varied and creative ideas on how to solve problems come best from people of varied backgrounds and experiences.

When you are hiring, you want to make sure that you have a range of ages represented. In addition, you want to have both men and women on your team. Women are becoming—and will continue to become—ever more instrumental in managing the family's finances. In fact, I insist that my clients bring in their spouse or partner when we have our annual meeting. It's not enough for their spouse to know who the advisor is; it's important that they know they are partners in making decisions.

DECISION TO PUT FAMILY FIRST

When interviewing candidates, I always ask about their families. In my opinion, how they interact with their families says a lot about them as people. Families always come first. Everyone on the team knows that they are expected to take care of their family needs first, and the rest of us will cover and pick up the slack, if necessary.

MANAGING THE TEAM

When you begin hiring people, your position changes. You are now not only responsible for your own work; you are also responsible for managing others. If you're going to lead the team, you have to understand what everybody's role is. You need to know how to market, how to be a rainmaker, and how to execute financial and estate planning processes. You need to know about banking and investment funds. You need to be able to delegate, but you first have to be able to do the job yourself.

BE A LEADER, NOT A DICTATOR

I hire smart people, and I empower them to challenge me and make their own decisions. I'm not a dictator. I'm a consensus builder. I don't know all the answers. I want everybody's input. But in the end, I'm the tie-breaker, and my team expects that from me.

LEAD BY EXAMPLE

I think the worst thing a leader can do is close the office door and be isolated from the team. A manager needs to be in the trenches with the team. I sit at a table with six other people, so I hire people I enjoy being with. They see and hear me on the phone talking to my clients all day. They see me dealing with issues. They see me come in every day, usually before they do, and at times leave after they do. They know I'm constantly thinking about the business and how to make it better for all of us. They know I'm right there with them.

PUT PEOPLE IN ROLES THAT PLAY
TO THEIR STRENGTHS

Do not set people up to fail by expecting them to do things they are ill-equipped to do. Don't expect your client associate to suddenly become a rainmaker. Hire outstanding people for their particular roles and let them do those jobs. That doesn't mean that you shouldn't expect everyone to pitch in when needed, but don't judge people for not being perfect at jobs they were never expected to do. Everyone should have a clearly defined primary role and also be comfortable with a secondary role. As new projects and issues come up, make sure everyone on the team knows who "owns" each one.

THE TEAM NEEDS TO ACT AS ONE, SO
YOU NEED TO BE ON THE SAME PAGE

I am not big on meetings, but you need to have a few regularly scheduled meetings to make sure everyone has the same information. We have a daily huddle to catch any problem early and to celebrate any successes. Weekly investment committee and marketing committee meetings make sure everyone is clear on our strategies. We are always transparent about processes and expectations, so there is never any question as to what is expected.

EVERYONE IS ACCOUNTABLE

I don't micromanage, but I keep track of what everyone is doing each day. Through our CRM system, I know exactly what each of our team members is focusing on.

We set lofty goals, so we track everything—new clients, lost clients, increased assets from current clients, decreased assets from current clients, etc.—and who was responsible for those accounts.

This isn't done in a punitive way. It is done so (1) we have a very current handle on the business, and (2) we can rectify small problems before they become large ones. (See sample tracking sheets in the appendix.)

BE STRUCTURED AND ORGANIZED

As your team expands, it's more important than ever to be organized so nothing falls through the cracks. It is unproductive to have meetings without a specific purpose, but these meetings can make all the difference between a smoothly functioning team and one that is scattered and unfocused.

MORNING HUDDLE

We begin every morning with a quick standing huddle where everyone goes over what they are doing that day. It's a quick way to see if there are going to be overlaps, or if something is being missed. It only takes a few minutes, but really sets the tone for the day.

MONDAY MORNING MEETING

This meeting is more structured than our daily huddle. Nikki, who is essentially our practice manager, provides an agenda. Each of us takes a turn outlining what is happening in our sphere of influence. These are quick, overview presentations, not deep dives. Greg will talk for five minutes about investment performance and any portfolio changes we might be considering. John will add to that. Daniel will then take a few minutes to highlight any technology or client issues and what is being done to address them. Jason will give an overview on his marketing activity, such as whom he's meeting with and events he might have planned. Lou will highlight a few fixed-income ideas that might make sense for certain clients. Brenna or Julie will provide a quick overview of what she is doing on the social media and promotions side of things. Nikki and Kristen will go over any office issues or initiatives. Finally, I'll weigh in with my ideas, tie everything together—and we're done. We start these meetings precisely at 8:30 a.m. and they typically end by 9:15 a.m.

Everyone leaves knowing what the goals for the week are and feeling like we are all rowing in the same direction.

INVESTMENT COMMITTEE MEETING

Every Monday afternoon, we have an investment committee meeting. Greg is responsible for constructing and managing the portfolios, but the committee is responsible for oversight. There are six of us on the committee: the three team partners, plus Greg, Daniel, and Luther, who is in New York. Greg will review the report he gave that morning and supply more detail. If somebody wants to bring an idea to the meeting, we'll discuss it at length and predict how that one change will affect the rest of the portfolio. What is the goal of the change? What is the predicted outcome? Will we end up overweight in a sector? Will we need to sell a group of equities to make room for the new suggestion? Are there any tax considerations to that sale? Will the change affect the portfolio risk-return profile? This meeting begins after the market closes.

PIPELINE MEETING

Every Wednesday, I meet with Jason to look at the pipeline in detail. We'll go over prospects and where they are in the development. He'll tell me his plan to move them to the next step, and I'll offer suggestions. If it would be helpful for me to meet with a prospect, we'll get that on my calendar. We'll also brainstorm ideas for meeting new prospects. We are always thinking of how to expand our universe of prospects. For every new prospecting event or activity, we'll do a cost-benefit analysis. How much will it cost? How much revenue will it bring in? When something doesn't work, Jason and I will go over our original assumptions and pinpoint what went wrong. Maybe the assumptions were wrong. Maybe something in the execution was at fault. Whatever the reason, we want to try and avoid it in the future. But a failure here or there doesn't stop us from continuing to try. You always want to be reaching out.

When this meeting is done, we both know what we need to do for the next week—which prospects to really focus on, which to keep in soft contact, which we want to approach on a first-time basis, what events to plan, etc. We come out of the meeting energized and ready to get to work.

QUARTERLY TEAM MEETING

We have a quarterly team meeting to go over the metrics of the business. At this meeting, we discuss our goals—including revenues, assets, and number of clients—and whether we fell short, met, or exceeded them. This meeting also gives everyone a chance to talk about big picture items that might not come up in the weekly update meetings. This meeting typically includes a dinner, where we hopefully celebrate another quarter well done, and get ready for the next.

RETAINING GOOD EMPLOYEES

Hiring outstanding employees is only the beginning of building your team. Once you have them onboard, you want to make sure they stay. Just as you want outstanding employees, they want an outstanding workplace. Providing that is in your control.

EMPOWER YOUR TEAM TO MAKE DECISIONS

If you hire good people, you have to allow them to grow in their roles and take ownership of responsibilities. This means you need to encourage them to come to you with suggestions, to challenge what you're doing, and to let them own a process. You need to give them the authority to do their jobs. You are undoubtedly giving them responsibilities, but responsibility without authority is a sure way to lose good people. I meet with my team regularly to get updates, but I do not micromanage them on a daily basis. I know how I like things handled, and it can be difficult to step away and trust that others can do things as well as I can. But if you don't give your team autonomy, you are basically trying to do everything yourself. You can't do everything yourself. I truly believe that my team makes me look a lot smarter than I am—which makes me think I did something well—which was to hire them in the first place.

MAKE THE OFFICE A PLACE
PEOPLE WANT TO COME TO

Your team will be spending most of their waking hours in the office. Make it a place where they are happy to be. We promote a family atmosphere, where we have fun and care about each other. We play pranks on each other. We celebrate birthdays, marriages, the birth of children, and other life milestones. We talk about what we did over the weekend and the things our children are doing. We offer help if it is needed. We treat each other like adults. That means if someone needs flexibility to take care of family responsibilities, such as getting kids to school or attending sports competitions, we don't think twice about it. Family always comes first. The benefit for the company is that these team members will stay for the long term because we make sure they know we respect and appreciate them.

NOT EVERY HIRE IS A GOOD FIT

Despite your best efforts, sometimes new hires don't work out. Don't let things drag on. It is in everyone's best interest to let the employee know sooner rather than later that it isn't working. The new hire is probably also unhappy and will now be able to find a more suitable job. I once had a team member who was really good at what he did, but he just didn't fit our culture. In our quarterly one-on-one, we talked about what he really wanted to do, because he was obviously unfulfilled. As we talked about his dream job, it became evident that he was more of a sole practitioner than a team player. I agreed to help him find a more suitable role in another organization, and he agreed to stay until we could hire a replacement. It worked for both of us, and we have remained friends to this day.

We also had a team member who had worked for us as a college intern and then joined us in a sales role. He came to me one day, almost in tears, and told me he just didn't think sales was for him. He thought I'd be mad.

I said, "Why would I be mad? I want you to be happy. If you're not happy doing a job, I don't take it personally. What would you like to do? Maybe I can help."

I wrote a glowing recommendation for him for one of the large investment firms, and he was running one of their divisions within four years. We are also still friends, because I didn't take his desire to move on personally.

Having someone not work out isn't the end of the world, but you don't want it to become a habit. Analyze your hiring process the same way you would a prospective investment. What did you miss that you want to make sure you see next time?

COMPENSATION

Advisors sometimes put off hiring people they need because they aren't sure how they will pay them. This concern can often be solved by approaching your firm. You'd be surprised how much it might be willing to provide. Many firms will provide a portion—or sometimes all—of a new team member's salary.

When it becomes clear that the practice could use another team member, I will put together a business plan illustrating the cost of the new position, as well as the potential benefits. I then approach my firm with this plan in hand. I will often offer to pay half the cost of the new hire if the firm would be willing to make an investment in the other half. When those making the decision go through the business plan and see how accretive the new position might be and also realize I'm willing to have skin in the game, they have rarely said no. I usually suggest that if, after a year, the investment doesn't meet return expectations, they can stop paying their part. Thankfully, that has never happened. I work for a firm that has been very fair with me. In return, I have treated them with respect and remained loyal.

Compensation and accountability are intertwined. Compensation is a reward and an incentive, but to earn it, team members must be held accountable for their goals. This concept is so important that I've hired coaches, and one in particular—Matt Oechsli—to help me get the accountability and compensation structures right.

I meet with each member of my team every three months to assess performance over the past quarter and to set goals for the new one. Frankly, because I am so particular in my hiring and everyone on the team is intimately involved in the day-to-day work of servicing our clients, I simply don't end up with people who have not met their goals. So, these meetings tend to be more about what else someone would like to take on. Do they want to take classes for additional certification? Do they think their work load has reached a point where it would make sense to hire another person? Do they see processes we could change to be more efficient? This is a meeting that really focuses on the team member rather than the team.

In addition to a base salary, I provide a quarterly bonus based on how the team is performing. Everyone on the team is eligible for a bonus, because they are all instrumental in the growth of the business. The bonus has two parts—how well the team does overall and how much each individual has contributed to that growth. The first part is comparable to profit sharing, while the second part is an incentive based on personal goals specific to each role. I also take 3 percent of the overall gross production and set it aside each year. This acts as a fifth bonus to all team members, paid at the end of December.

The purpose of a bonus structure is to make sure those who are helping you grow your business are fairly compensated. This isn't the time to be frugal. On a percentage basis, my team members have seen their year-over-year compensation grow faster than my own. They know I mean it when I say I wouldn't be where I am without them.

When my long-term assistant was getting ready to retire, she told me her bonus was too large. This was her last year, so I didn't need to incentivize her to remain. We both knew she would continue to provide outstanding service to me and our clients whether she received a bonus or not. Her work ethic was unparalleled.

I told her I wasn't paying her nearly enough. "How can I put a price tag on loyalty? You've been with me for twenty-seven years."

I always ask team members for feedback in regard to their compensation. I let them know that I think what they are earning makes sense, but I want to hear from them, as well. I feel it is important to be generous with your staff. Even when the practice was just starting out, I felt like I was generous with my staff. Treating your team well builds loyalty.

SUCCESSION

When you are growing a business, the last thing you are thinking about is who should take over when you are no longer there. In fact, surveys have consistently found that fewer than half of the corporations and firms in the United States have a specific succession plan in place for the eventual departure of the CEO.

If you have equal partners, they need to be part of the conversation, and there should be a specific agreement in place that covers all contingencies. If you own the business outright, then you have a little more leeway in designating someone to take over the business.

No matter what your succession plan, it is good management to have one. As a team leader or owner of a company, you owe it to your team and clients to assure the continuation of the business. It's part of being a good CEO.

HOW TO DEAL WITH YOUR HOME OFFICE

Your firm is there to help you. When you do well, it does well. So, don't hesitate to ask for help if you need it. Over the years, I've developed a close relationship with my firm. There are a couple of things I am always aware of, however, when presenting a proposition:

1. Don't be a greedy—Don't ask for more than you need or for something you aren't going to use.

2. Be respectful—Don't assume your firm owes you something. Don't come across as entitled. When I ask my firm for something, I often offer to cover half the cost. They really love this and are more apt to say yes if you are willing to put some of your own skin in the game.

GET TO KNOW THE PEOPLE AT HEADQUARTERS

Most major firms and some independents have people who handle research, wealth management, due diligence on separately managed accounts, insurance, estate management, syndications, fixed income, and every other area of finance. Get to know the specialists you work with. Go to dinner. Send thank-you notes. Invite them to appreciation dinners.

Develop a close relationship with your manager. Managers can make or break a career. Pick up the phone. Have a conversation once a week to develop a rapport. Keep him or her in the loop on what your business is doing. I have been very fortunate that I have a manager who has believed in me and my team for the past twenty years.

Have a full-fledged business plan. Show your manager your business plan so he or she knows your goals. Managers appreciate that. We have created our own brand—a boutique business with thirteen people providing high-level service—within the confines of a global, world-class financial powerhouse. I have one-, three-, and five-year goals—and my manager knows exactly what those are.

MAKE IT A TWO-WAY STREET

Your firm wants you to succeed, so it will be happy to provide you with resources. In return, you need to provide them with results. Develop a relationship of trust. Don't tell them you can do something if you can't deliver—do what you say. And don't bad-mouth anyone. But be open and honest about those who aren't pulling their weight and areas where they need to improve. And, importantly, always be willing to help. If you have a great idea, share it with others. If you are generous with your time and ideas, the firm is going to want to be generous back.

My firm has always been generous with me because I've developed good, mutually respectful relationships with my manager, the heads of the divisions, and the presidents. I've also made it a two-way street. If they ask me to come to Boston or New York and speak in front of the office or help a younger person, I'm happy to do so. By working together, the firm and your business can both grow.

KEY TAKEAWAYS

- Be smart about who you hire—they are representing you.

- Make sure you're working with people who want to learn and who get along well with others.

- Hire good people, then let them do their jobs.

CHAPTER 8
MISTAKES ADVISORS MAKE—AND SOME I'VE MADE MYSELF

WARREN BUFFETT HAS been quoted as saying, "You only have to do a very few things right in your life so long as you don't do too many things wrong." Unfortunately, no one is perfect, so we are all going to do some things wrong. We can, however, minimize the number of things we do wrong if we are aware of some of the more common mistakes.

LETTING OTHERS FRAME WHO YOU ARE

Early in my career, I was really focused on the sales part of the business. At that time, there was less emphasis on estate planning, insurance, banking, lending and credit, and comprehensive wealth management. I was more of an old-fashioned stock and bond broker. I convinced people to give me a shot and then tried to purchase stocks and municipal bonds that earned a good rate of return for my clients. Developing relationships often took the form of communicating the firm's research, calling and pitching the client on each idea I thought was appropriate, and becoming friends with my prospects and clients—just being someone they liked to get together with. During this time, there was one client with whom I had a particularly good relationship. He was an aggressive trader, and it seemed like everything I did for him worked. He made a lot of money on my suggestions. This relationship worked outside of the office, as well. He always invited me to play in his charity golf tournaments and insisted on playing with me—not so much because I was a good golfer (I'm really not), but because I was his guy and made him laugh. During this time, he gave me a few referrals that turned out to be good long-term clients. We were buddies.

Over time, I watched him take his company public, and our relationship only got better—or so I thought. After a couple of years, his company was acquired. He came into several hundred million dollars. I had set myself up nicely and was looking forward to advising him on his newfound wealth. But as it turns out, I'd jumped the gun. I will never forget when some of the top people at my firm and I came in for a presentation. He started the meeting singing my praises and telling everyone how wonderful I was. A few days after the meeting, he told me that he gave 90 percent of his proceeds to another firm, which was going to take care of his estate planning and comprehensive wealth management, and basically act as a quasi-family office. "But don't worry," he told me. "You will still get most of my fun money."

So, there it was; I was his "fun money" guy! I had never been so embarrassed and angry in my business career. It became obvious that he didn't take me seriously. Perhaps it was my lack of experience, but I truly believe it was because he didn't see me as a serious professional. Whatever it was, I obviously wasn't proactive enough to convince him that I (or my firm) had a real understanding of what it took to be a wealth management professional.

From that day forward, I vowed to educate myself on estate planning and comprehensive wealth management and become less of a salesman and more of a partner with my clients. Instead of appealing to their greed, I would appeal to their need! Ray Sclafani, a well-known coach in the industry, wrote about reinventing yourself and not allowing your clients to frame you in *You've Been Framed: How to Reframe Your Wealth Management Business and Renew Client Relationships*. It resonated with me because that is exactly what I did early in my career when I moved from being the "fun money" guy to the knowledgeable and expert professional, albeit a professional who still knew how to have fun.

Clients will often frame an advisor as their "bond expert" or "insurance expert" or "large cap equity guy," or some other specialized expert. If you want to specialize, that's fine. But if you want to do comprehensive wealth management planning and raise some serious assets, you don't want to be pigeonholed as the equities person or the fixed-income person, or the "fun money" guy. You have to reframe your image in the mind of your client.

Clients will identify you by how you frame yourself. If you describe yourself and your team as providing advice, planning, and wealth management services, they'll look at you a little differently than if you describe yourself as a broker, or just an equities or bond manager. Don't sell yourself short.

Sclafani notes that "the second reframe of top advisory firms is that they have stopped *selling* to their clients and started *partnering* with their clients."[16] That is exactly what I was forced to do many years before the book was written. I stopped just selling my investment services and learned to partner with clients in all aspects of their wealth management.

---

16   Sclafani, *You've Been Framed: How to Reframe Your Wealth Management Business.*

BEING UNPREPARED

I once received a referral for a prospect in another state. Let's call him Sam Jones. His firm had been acquired by another, and a few of the executives on the acquiring firm's board were my clients. They had recommended my services to the board members at the acquired firm. I followed up the referral, and Sam asked to meet in person at his house. This was during the time in my career when I was still specializing in helping executives deal with their restricted stock and options needs, and the merging of the two firms had brought some of these issues to the forefront.

So, I scheduled a meeting, booked a flight, and didn't think much more about it. After I arrived in town, I rented a car at the airport and pulled out a map to route myself (believe it or not, there were no cell phones or internet at that point). It was a good thing I was still in the parking lot, because I think I would have run off the road if I'd been reading the map while driving. There, running north to south through this medium-sized city, was Sam Jones Boulevard.

It turns out he was a well-known businessman, philanthropist, and supporter of the local university, where the business college was named for him. So was, obviously, the main thoroughfare. This was no mere corporate executive. This was a very wealthy man who was willing to talk to me about managing some of his assets. I was totally unprepared.

I got myself to the meeting and was met by a surprisingly young man. I decided to just be straight with him, "Sam, I'm sorry. I didn't know you were this much of a big deal." He laughed at the comment and I got lucky and turned it into an advantage because I was able to ask him about himself. I particularly asked him to tell me about his philanthropic endeavors and what it meant to him to be able to give back. We had a great conversation and then got down to business.

He appreciated my interest in his life and his passions—not just his money—and gave me some of his assets to manage. That account eventually grew over time. After he passed, his son took over, and I still do business with the next generation.

Things could have gone very differently, however. I was unprepared for the prospect I was meeting. I had lumped him into a group instead of viewing him as an individual. I never made that mistake again. In today's technological age, it is easy to find information on anybody. Before a meeting, do as much research as you can on the people who will be present. The prospect/client will be impressed that you did your homework and will appreciate your thoroughness. Attention to detail in this business will set you apart.

When other professionals want to do business with me, I appreciate the fact that someone takes the time and effort to do research on me before we meet. All things being equal, I'm more likely to do business with that person than with someone who doesn't make that effort. In turn, I do my homework on those I want as clients because I think it is a sign of respect. If I want someone to give me business, the least I can do is show that I've done my homework, the same way I expect those who want to work with me to do their homework on me.

HIDING UNDERLYING EXPENSES

We've talked about fees in a previous chapter, but a mistake I see advisors make over and over again is not making all fees and expenses clear to their clients. They quote a management fee but fail to note that there are also fees and expenses related to the underlying investments. Once clients discover this, they lose trust in that advisor and begin to look for another.

A while back, I met with a prospect who had called me out of the blue. When we started talking expenses, I asked what his current advisor was charging. He confidently told me, "I'm paying eighty basis points."

But when I looked at the portfolio, I saw that he owned several mutual funds that were charging over one hundred basis points of operating expenses. In addition, he was paying a lot more for the class of shares he owned than institutional shares would have cost him, yet he knew nothing of this. He really thought all he was paying was the advisory fee. Typically, clients believe the advisor has negotiated a discount with the underlying funds, if they think about it at all.

I make sure that clients understand exactly what they are paying. "Here is what our firm is going to charge you, and I receive half of that." And if there are any underlying fees for any mutual funds, ETFs, etc., I spell them out. I make sure they know there is nothing underhanded about these additional fees, but it is important that they understand they are paying them.

Many times, when I point out the true costs, clients say, "My advisor never told me that." Then, they want to move their account. Rightly or wrongly, they believe that if their advisor isn't being straight about expenses, they might be hiding other things, as well.

IGNORING THE SPOUSE AND CHILDREN

Typically, one spouse dominates the investing. It's rare to see both spouses have an equal interest. However, it is a mistake to work solely with the more interested partner.

If I have four meetings per year with a client, I insist that at least one of those meetings includes both spouses. This is in addition to communicating with both of them throughout the course of the year. I mentioned earlier that 70 percent of surviving spouses and 66 percent of surviving children move their inherited wealth to a new advisor.[17] That's not because they don't like or trust the advisor the primary investor used. It's because they don't know them.

Just as you involve the spouse so he or she gets to know you and understand their investments, you want to include the next generation as early as possible, as long as your client gives you permission, of course. If the children are still young, you can begin by simply showing an interest. Learn the names and birth dates of your clients' children. Ask about them regularly. Know where they are going to college or where they are working. Then, when they get into their twenties and thirties, encourage your client to bring them into the financial wealth management picture. Begin to ask questions to start a conversation: "What do they know about what you have? How can I help them?"

The best way to help is by opening accounts for the children. This will allow you to form relationships with them as discrete individuals, as opposed to extensions of their parents. Typically, I open the account because I'm their parents' contact, but then I turn them over to a younger member of my team to be in regular communication.

IGNORING YOUR CLIENTS' CENTERS OF INFLUENCE

Your clients undoubtedly work with CPAs and attorneys, as well as real estate brokers, bankers, and other professionals. These are all people you need to develop relationships with, because they exert influence on your clients' lives. It is not unusual for CPAs to

---

17   Skinner, op. cit.; Polyak, op. cit.

recommend that a client change investment advisors to one the CPA knows better.

When you obtain a new client, ask if you can speak with the client's other professionals: "Do you have a CPA you've worked with for a while and are comfortable with? Do you have an estate planning attorney that you've worked with for a while and are comfortable with?" If the answer is yes, ask, "Do you mind if I give that person a call and introduce myself?"

When people take on a new advisor, their current professionals often wonder if that new advisor is a threat. Are they going to suggest new CPAs and attorneys, as well? They will then sometimes actively work to undercut your influence with the client to protect their own.

I stop this very common dynamic in its tracks by building relationships with their current centers of influence. After I receive permission from the client, I simply pick up the phone and call. Most advisors don't think to do this. I didn't either earlier in my career. If you are calling their CPA, simply say, "Mike and Diane opened up an account recently with me. They gave their permission for me to speak with you. I just want to introduce myself and ensure that I'm being as tax-efficient as possible with their investments. Are there any tax considerations I should be aware of, so I make sure I don't trigger something?"

I have just begun working with some new clients who have recently retired. Even though they have substantial assets, they're not in the highest tax bracket anymore. However, all of their fixed income was in tax-free instruments. That might not be the most efficient way to invest their capital now that they are in a lower bracket. These are things I could discuss with their CPA that would not only help me invest sensibly for my client, but reassure the CPA that he or she was going to remain a part of this client's wealth management team.

In addition, centers of influence are one of the best sources of referrals. Once they know you are not a threat, they are more apt to refer business to you. Stay in front of them four times per year and you will be surprised at how valuable they can be to your business.

TALKING TOO MUCH

Advisors often try to impress clients with how much they know. Your clients will tune you out if you make meetings all about you. Instead of dominating a meeting, do 10 percent of the talking and 90 percent of the listening. Let your clients speak. Let your prospects speak. Ask open-ended questions. Don't pretend to know an answer if you do not know it. Tell them you're not sure, but you'll find the answer, or you'll find the best resource to get the answer.

Recently, a new prospect came in. One of the first questions I asked was, "How do you feel about money?" I then let him talk. When he was finished, I asked a series of follow-up questions: "Tell me what keeps you up at night. Tell me what you worry about with your existing portfolio. Tell me what you're looking for in an ideal advisor. Tell me how your philosophy differs from your spouse's. If it's much different, how do we come to a balance that's right for both of you? What are your goals with your assets? Do you wish to leave as much as you can to your children, or do you want to leave them only a certain amount and leave the rest to charity?"

Advisors also take too long to explain their investment philosophy. You should be able to explain it in about a minute. Thirty seconds is better. After that, your clients can ask as many questions as they like. Droning on about your philosophy and making it more complicated than it is will not impress a client.

In fact, speaking too much is a sign of nervousness and inexperience. That is not the image you want to project.

NOT ASKING FOR THE BUSINESS

Dancing around the elephant in the room is a massive mistake for a marketing person. Everyone knows why you are having a meeting. You want the business. So, ask for it. I have people ask me to lunch. I might know they want to sell me something, but I resent it if they frame the invitation as a social gathering. I'd much rather an insurance salesman say, "Hi, Sal. I'd like to have lunch with you and review your current insurance coverage. If you're comfortable where you are, fine. If not, I'd like an opportunity to help and provide you with a better insurance solution. That's my ultimate goal. Are you open to that?"

Advisors often avoid saying what they really want. I think they believe if they ask, they might hear no, and that will be the end. So they avoid asking. Instead, they often just meet with prospects and chat. It feels like they are just checking the box. Their manager expects them to have a set number of lunch meetings each month, and this checks that box of another lunch. Afterward, they believe they had a productive meeting because everyone had a good time. But the prospect is no closer to being a client than he or she was before the meeting.

Some advisors will have lunch with a prospect four to six times and never ask for their business. This is a waste of time! Don't be one of those advisors. Tell your prospects what your goals are right up front. I think it's a breath of fresh air to people.

NOT HAVING AN OPINION

You are an advisor. By definition, you need to have opinions. How else are you going to advise? You need to be well-read and up to date on the most recent investment research. You also need to have an opinion on what that research means for your clients. But no one is an expert on everything. If a question is outside your expertise, be ready to provide the firm's viewpoint, as well as that of other respected strategists. For example, a client asked my opinion about investing in a German company. This is not an area in which I feel comfortable providing investment advice. However, I know where to get an opinion I respect, so I told the client I would get him specific research, along with the informed opinion of specialists in European investing. Providing this information is what clients are paying you for.

IGNORING THE FUTURE

The industry is changing. It is very different today than it was twenty-five years ago when I started. And it will be very different twenty-five years from now. We ignore those changes at our peril. But those changes can be a source of opportunity, as well as danger. In the next chapter, we'll examine some of the major trends and how you can position your team to take advantage of them.

KEY TAKEAWAYS

- Don't let others frame you.

- Failing to prepare is preparing to fail.

- Be transparent on fees.

- Pay attention to your clients' centers of influence.

CHAPTER 9
KEEPING UP WITH A CHANGING INDUSTRY

I HAVE SEEN a lot of changes in the financial services industry since I started more than twenty-five years ago. At that time, there was no internet or email. Data and research were scarce and difficult to access. Clients were certainly less educated and knowledgeable about investment strategies, but so were their advisors. There were fewer products and, if we're being frank, less fiduciary focus on the needs of the clients and more focus on profits for the firms. We were often more stockbroker than wealth advisor.

Much has changed since then. Technological advances, which have made it possible to transmit information in the blink of an eye, have changed the way we connect with clients, as well as how and when we connect. Not so long ago, the main scarcity was information. In fact, clients used to call us in the middle of the day for quotes on their stock positions. They lacked the data to make informed financial decisions. The challenge today isn't a lack of data and research. It is sorting through all that is available, condensing it into digestible bites, and interpreting it for our clients. Those clients often have access to much of this research themselves via the internet, so they come in much more educated about investments and portfolios. They aren't looking to us for the data—they are looking to us for advice on what all that data means. They are looking for help on properly processing everything. They expect transparency, and they expect us to be a fiduciary for their wealth.

Many of these trends—particularly in technology—will continue to impact the industry for the foreseeable future. In addition, new trends that we can't foresee will undoubtedly appear. To prepare for the unknown, it helps to look at the trends we see today, focus on setting up our businesses to take advantage of what we can, and adapt to what we can't.

CHANGING DEMOGRAPHICS

Traditionally, this business has been primarily composed of young to middle-aged men advising and connecting with middle-aged to older men. Today, that is changing quickly.

Women already control more than half the private wealth in the United States and are expected to control two-thirds by 2020.[18] Women are creating their own wealth as entrepreneurs and C-suite executives. Wives are no longer content to be silent partners.

This trend is playing out in my own practice. If I am dealing with clients in their seventies, I am most likely working with the patriarch. Their wives rarely want to know what decisions are being made on their and their family's behalf. For clients in their sixties, I'd estimate 30 percent have both spouses equally involved. One or the other might be a little more interested and active, but both are involved in the decisions and want to be kept informed on changes in their portfolio. That percentage increases with each decade, until we get to those in their thirties, where nearly all decisions are made

---

18   Malito, "Women are about to control a massive amount of wealth but can't find anyone to manage it."

equally by both spouses. For this age group, if one spouse is more active than the other, it can just as easily be the wife as the husband.

This increase in female decision-makers is creating a sea of change in how financial planners are dealing with clients. Studies have shown that women invest differently than men.[19] They tend to trade less, and they are more risk averse. They want to know the reasoning behind investment decisions. As a result, women often get better results. I enjoy working with women because they tend to be more patient. They are typically better long-term investors, which fits with my investment philosophy.

In addition, the younger generations are becoming involved in their family wealth—or creating their own wealth—sooner than ever before. Coming of age during the financial crisis, this group is well aware that nothing is guaranteed, and they understand the need for investing and planning, though they are often leery of banks and formal financial services.

Finally, within the next thirty years, we will see about $30 trillion of wealth moving from today's baby boomers to their children and grandchildren, the groups dubbed Generation X and millennials.[20] These cohorts, particularly the millennials, have a very different outlook on life than their parents. They want to know why their advisors are doing the things they are. They want to be part of the decision-making. They often want their investments to be doing good while doing well. A survey by the Oppenheimer Funds found that 33 percent of wealthy millennials expect to incorporate environmental, social, and governance standards, as well as impact investments, in their family's portfolio.[21] And they want things to happen quickly.

---

19   Low, "Are Women Better Investors Than Men? Here's What The Studies Say."
20   PwC United States, "Managing millennial money."
21   OppenheimerFunds & Campden Wealth Research, "Coming of Age: The Investment Behaviors of Ultra-High Net Worth Millennials in North America."

To connect with this dynamic, diverse group of clients, advisors need to make sure their staff is just as dynamic and diverse. My team is made up of men and women ranging in age from twenty-three to sixty-five. This means that every client can find someone on staff with whom they feel comfortable, and with whom they connect. In my opinion, this makes a considerable difference.

I recently met with one of my female clients, who has two daughters in their thirties. I told her that I'd really like to meet her daughters. We had just helped one of them with a mortgage, and we have trust accounts that the mother operates for the benefit of her children. I told her that I had younger team members who do a great job working with the next generation, and it would be beneficial to her daughters to meet and get to know them. She thought having her daughters meet with my team was a great idea, and so did her daughters. They are now working with a couple of the thirty-year-olds on my team, who think the way they do. I have no doubt the daughters will be long-term clients, because we have made the effort to adjust to their needs, rather than try to have them conform to a model that worked for their parents or grandparents.

TECHNOLOGY

It seems obvious to note that technology is going to play a large part in the wealth management of the future—it's already embedded in the wealth management of today—but the difference between today and tomorrow is in *how* technology will be perceived. It will no longer be a "nice to have" or something that sets you apart from your peers. Being able to provide digital offerings for your clients will be a "must have," because your clients will not only be demanding it, but expecting it. It's like having a good roof on your house. No buyer will offer more for the house because the roof doesn't leak—that's just expected. What they will do, however, is walk away from a house with a leaky roof because they wonder what else might be wrong with the house. This will be the default for financial advisors in the future. No one will think an advisor is cutting edge because they use the most up-to-date technology. That will be expected. Instead, they'll walk away if the advisor doesn't use it, because it will make them doubt the advice, as well.

Younger generations, in particular, will be expecting their advisors to be technologically savvy. But they won't just be looking at the software used to help design portfolios. They'll be looking at technology to connect with their advisor. This group has grown up with the internet, instant messages, texts, online dating, FaceTime, streaming entertainment, and all the other ways of digitally connecting. Thus, they prefer to communicate digitally rather than in person.

This preference for digital interaction has given rise to the growing robo advisor industry. This model uses an algorithmic method to manage money. Fill in a few fields related to age and how much you want to invest, and it provides a standard balanced portfolio. Younger investors are using these platforms rather than traditional advisors because they are cost efficient and, in the investors' minds, provide an investment model that is just as good as those touted by financial planners.

In this same vein, clients have embraced technology to do their own research and make their own investment decisions. With everyone having access to the same data, it is challenging to consistently beat traditional benchmarks. What this means is that portfolio management alone is becoming digitalized and commoditized. For this reason, to grow your business, you will need to find ways other than investment performance to set yourself apart from other advisors. To justify charging for your services, you must offer comprehensive wealth management, focus on both sides of a client's balance sheet, and provide incomparable service.

Although robo advisors have their appeal to younger investors, it is important to note their downside. Cybersecurity is a real concern when dealing with millions of dollars. The clients of elite advisors might be very comfortable online, but they also recognize the need to have their assets custodied at a firm they deem safe.

Knowing that your clients are comfortable with digital communication doesn't mean you should abandon face-to-face interactions, however. I still reach out and call every one of my clients. In addition, I meet with my clients. I break bread with them. Younger generations might say they prefer to connect via text, email, or our investment portal, but we think it's important that they understand the value of good, old-fashioned eye contact. Nothing beats sharing a meal and talking about life to cement a relationship.

FEE COMPRESSION AND COMPETITION

A couple of years ago, Heidrick & Struggles put together a digital working group to help the financial services industry prepare for the future. The report they came up with outlines the effect of technology on how advisors and firms are currently developing and delivering financial advice, and how this practice will evolve in the future.[22] This digital advice group doesn't possess a crystal ball, but they agreed that consumer comfort with online investment opportunities will be much higher than it is today, which seems like a pretty safe prediction. What they also foresaw, which might have more of an impact on financial planning firms, is that the advances in technology will

---

22   Roeder, "The Future of Digital Financial Advice."

result in lower investment management margins, because consumers will demand greater value at lower costs.

We've already seen the beginnings of this compression. It wasn't that long ago that the typical advisor was charging between 1 percent and 3 percent commission per transaction. This then dropped to $0.10 per share, which fell to $0.05 per share, which fell to nothing per share as we transition to a fee-based model on assets for advice. Similarly, the management fees have also compressed over time as technology has improved.

Investors simply want to make sure they are getting value for their money. Meeting this demand doesn't mean we have to have a race to the bottom in terms of fees, but it does mean we have to provide value that the clients believe is worth the cost. Those firms that use a "set and forget" model are going to have a difficult time competing in a world where consumers can do that themselves.

REGULATIONS

It's no secret that the wealth management industry is heavily regulated. Look at any investment research report or fund prospectus, and you'll see hundreds of words of disclaimer copy. But the one rule that sent shock waves through the industry hasn't even been adopted—though the debate around it made the word *fiduciary* a household noun.

The Department of Labor (DOL) Fiduciary Rule proposal put the typical advisory business model, in which advisors sell their firm's products to clients, under a spotlight.[23] Clients, consumers, and regulators are demanding that these business relationships be more transparent. They want guarantees that those products are actually

---

23   KPMG, "Evolving Investment Management Regulation: Succeeding in an uncertain landscape."

appropriate for the client's individual situation. And if advisors are suggesting changes in investments, they want guarantees that those changes are actually needed and are not just a way for the advisor to earn a commission.

The DOL Fiduciary Rule has been tabled at the time of this writing, but the debate put the idea of fiduciary standards squarely in the middle of the relationship between advisor and client.

CONSOLIDATION

While many of the advances in the industry have been beneficial to the client, they have been less kind to advisory firms. Advances in technology have made gathering data and modeling portfolios more efficient, but, in the process, they have reduced the number of jobs available in the industry. That means there likely will be industry-wide consolidation and contraction. Marginal advisors will leave the business, while bigger and better teams that have positioned themselves as solution providers rather than product salespeople will be the ones that will not only survive, but thrive in a more competitive, professional environment.

ADAPT OR DIE

Sometimes we get so swept up in day-to-day life that we forget to look into the future and prepare ourselves for it. While we can't forecast exactly what the future will bring, we can do some things right now to make sure your practice continues to grow.

USE TECHNOLOGY TO YOUR ADVANTAGE

Technology can be used to lower your costs while expanding your offerings. Computer programs excel at completing repetitive tasks, which frees you to concentrate on more advanced tasks, as well as on rainmaking and building relationships with your clients.

Despite its ability to streamline a number of investment processes, it is doubtful that technology will ever completely replace the individualized decisions needed for true wealth management. Even as artificial intelligence moves into the mainstream, there will always be areas in which the human advisor excels. Digital platforms are not likely to surpass humans in their ability to build relationships or create client-tailored solutions for unique situations. By doubling down on those areas where humans excel— sharpening soft skills, building deeper relationships, and expanding client networks— wealth advisors can increase their readiness for future trends.[24]

EMBRACE CHANGING DEMOGRAPHICS

The easiest way to handle changing demographics is to make sure your team reflects these changes. You want your team to hold similar values and support a consistent investment philosophy, but beyond that, the more varied the better. In fact, studies have shown that workforce diversity can bring about an increase in productivity and competitive advantages.[25] Diverse firms have the potential of offering more solutions to clients because of new ideas and processes brought into the organization. In addition, workplace diversity increases employee morale and energizes employees to work more effectively and efficiently.[26]

---

24   Roeder, op. cit.

25   Green, et. al., "Diversity in the Workplace: Benefits, Challenges, and the Required Managerial Tools."

26   Ibid.

MAINTAIN YOUR OLD-FASHIONED VALUES

- Break bread with your prospects and clients.

- Find ways to have face-to-face communications.

- Plan events and activities to show appreciation.

- Surround your clients with the bear hug of structural alpha.

There is a reason "old-fashioned" values have continued to play a role in business through the years. Humans simply have a need to connect with other humans. No amount of demographic change or technological advancements will alter this fact. In the future, everyone will use software to make portfolio allocation and data analysis more efficient. To set yourself apart and make yourself attractive to wealthy clients, you need to make sure your technology-based business is also people-based.

ALWAYS ASK, "WHAT'S NEXT?"

We are in the midst of constant change. You always have to think ahead and ask yourself, "What's next?" so you can make sure you sail with rising tides—not get washed away by them. Today, our team is dynamic and diverse, so we're better positioned to handle potential changes on the horizon. The future is evolving—and I can't wait to see what comes next.

KEY TAKEAWAYS

- Build diversity within your business to better embrace change.

- Always think one step ahead.

- Use structural alpha to build client satisfaction and loyalty.

CONCLUSION

HINTS AND TIPS TO GROW A WEALTH MANAGEMENT BUSINESS

ACCORDING TO EXTENSIVE RESEARCH from the Oechsli Institute, there are fourteen criteria the affluent want addressed in their relationship with their financial advisor.[27] When looking back on all that I've learned during my decades-long career, I realize I've stumbled onto many of these fourteen points through trial and error.

When I started writing this book, my intent was to provide a compendium of actionable, time-tested activities that financial advisors could incorporate into their own practices to grow an elite wealth management business without having to experience the errors I sometimes made. I think I've accomplished that. So, instead of putting together a long conclusion, I thought it would be most helpful to aggregate the hints and tips I've presented in one place, starting with chapter 2. I hope you find them useful and refer back to them when you need new ideas for improving your rainmaking, providing service to clients, or building your team.

And if you have your own hints and techniques, I'd love to hear them. This industry works best when we work together and share ideas on how to serve clients best.

---

27   Oechsli Institute with First Clearing, "Best Practices of Today's Elite Advisors Oechsli."

CRITERIA THE AFFLUENT WANT ADDRESSED IN A FINANCIAL ADVISOR / CLIENT RELATIONSHIP

—with credit to the Oechsli Institute

COMMUNICATION

1. Listening and understanding their family's needs.
2. Being trustworthy.
3. Possessing breadth and depth of industry knowledge.
4. Being a problem solver.
5. Providing personal and timely, not mechanical communication.
6. Overseeing family's financial affairs, not marketing.
7. Delivering high-level personal service.

FINANCIAL SERVICES

1. Meeting investment performance expectations.
2. Protecting investments from downside risk.
3. Making them fully aware of fees on an annual basis.
4. Helping create a financial plan and keeping it current.
5. Using current technology for access and reporting.
6. Coordinating and organizing their financial documents.
7. Providing insurance solutions.

CHAPTER 2: TOP TEN 10 KEYS TO SUCCESS

- Educate yourself.
- Think like an entrepreneur (because you are one!)
- It's all about people.
- This business is difficult; don't give up.
- Have a game plan.
- Play to your strengths.

- Be professional/trustworthy.

- You can't do it all alone.

- Practice what you preach.

- Stay humble.

CHAPTER 3: RAINMAKING— BUILDING A PIPELINE

- Have and use a good CRM system.

- Always be prepared.

- Believe you are going to succeed.

- Have alligator skin.

- Cast a very narrow but deep net.

- Become an expert so prospects want to talk with you.

- Ask for introductions to specific people.

- Work to make referrals the foundation of your pipeline.

- Set up a professional networking group composed of centers of influence.

- Ask top producers to let you work with the bottom percentage of their book.

CHAPTER 4: RAINMAKING—CONVERTING PROSPECTS INTO CLIENTS

- Differentiate yourself—be an expert.

- Be professionally persistent.

- Build a relationship based on your ability to provide information prospects want.

- Host small, intimate educational events.

- Speak less, listen more.

- Be straightforward and transparent—ask for the business.

- Ask a series of questions that illicit a "yes" response.

- Dress appropriately.

- Be a great storyteller.

CHAPTER 5: USING STRUCTURAL ALPHA TO BECOME INDISPENSABLE

- Treat your clients like family.

- Set up a consistent contact schedule.

- Keep in regular contact with your clients/send research reports and articles of interest.

- Surprise and delight your clients.

- Get in front of bad news. Deliver it as soon as possible and have a solution ready.

- Be available.

- Connect with the professionals who are important to your clients

- Become an expert in other centers of influences.

- Provide education for clients, children, and spouses.

CHAPTER 6: YOUR WEALTH MANAGEMENT STRATEGY

- Have a simple investment philosophy.

- Don't compete on investment strategy alone.

- Invest in stability--not fads.

- Be able to communicate your philosophy.

- Execute it consistently and systematically.

- Provide educational resources for your clients so they can act as true partners in their own financial decisions.

- Always make sure your clients know you are acting in their best interests.

CHAPTER 7: YOU CAN'T DO IT ALONE— BUILDING AND MANAGING A TEAM

- Use your firm's resources as a virtual team.

- Use your firm and contacts to recruit people to your personal team.

- Take your time when hiring.

- Be a leader, not a dictator.

- Lead by example.

- Be structured and organized.

- Empower your team to make their own decisions.

- Make the office a place people want to come to.

- Have a succession plan.

CHAPTER 8: MISTAKES ADVISORS MAKE—AND SOME I'VE MADE MYSELF

- Be friendly, but stay professional.

- Be prepared.

- Reveal all expenses.

- Pay attention your client's centers of influence.

- Listen much more than you talk.

- Ask for the business.

- Form and share your opinions.

- Plan for the future.

CHAPTER 9: KEEPING UP WITH A CHANGING INDUSTRY

- Make use of technology.

- Embrace changing demographics.

- Act in your clients' best interest.

- Always ask, "What's next?"

ABOUT THE AUTHOR

SAL TIANO is a Managing Director and co-head of the Tiano, Armour & Smyth Wealth Managers at J.P. Morgan Securities, which was ranked on the 2019 "Top 50 Private Wealth Advisor Teams in the Country" list by *Barron's*. The Tiano, Armour & Smyth team is one of the largest teams at J.P. Morgan Securities, with thirteen professionals managing billions of dollars in client assets from a clientele comprised primarily of entrepreneurs, corporate executives, and retirees. Sal, who has generated well over $100 million in revenue during his career, was ranked second in South Florida on the *Forbes* "Best-In-State Wealth Advisors" list in 2019,[1] as well as listed on its 2018 "Top 100 Financial Advisors in America"[2] list. He has also found himself on "Best of" lists published by the *Financial Times*,[3] and was ranked among the top ten financial advisors in Florida by *Barron's*,[4] which also ranked him on their 2019 "Top 100 Advisors in the Country" list.

---

1   *Forbes*, "Best-In-State Wealth Advisors."
2   *Forbes*, "Top Wealth Advisors." June 30, 2018, accessed March 29, 2019, https://www.forbes.com/top-wealth-advisors/#5ef1c7e61a14.
3   Financial Times, "FT 400 Top Financial Advisers 2017 listing."
4   Garmhausen, "Highlights From Barron's 2018 Top 1,200 Financial Advisors Ranking."

Sal began his career in 1989 with Drexel Burnham Lambert and joined J.P. Morgan Securities' predecessor firm in 1991, where he became one of the youngest Senior Managing Directors in the history of the company. A graduate of Dartmouth College, Sal has served as the co-head agent of the class of 1988, as well as the chair of Friends of Dartmouth Hockey. In addition to his wealth management career, Sal founded Pure Hockey in 2002 with a business partner. The company, which originated with a single location, is now the largest hockey retailer in the country, with fifty-four locations in eighteen states and more than a thousand employees. Sal incorporates this entrepreneurial spirit in his wealth management practice, as it allows him to better understand the complex and varying needs of his clients.

Beyond his business career, Sal is known throughout the Greater Palm Beach area for his support of multiple charities and community groups. He serves on the Planned Giving Council for Place of Hope, a child welfare organization in Palm Beach County; is a co-founder of the Jimmy Martello Foundation, a charitable organization set up in memory of a close friend who died in the World Trade Center tragedy; serves on the board of The Benjamin School, where he currently chairs the Investment Committee; and is a Trustee of the foundation board of Jupiter Medical Center, where he is on the investment and finance committees.

Sal lives in Jupiter, Florida, with his wife, Kim, and their five children. He enjoys golf, coaching, and working with children.

APPENDIX
SAMPLE LOG SHEETS

1. NEW CLIENT LOG

2. NEW ASSET LOG

3. CLIENT LOSS LOG

4. FEE ASSETS LOG

5. ASSET FLOW SUMMARY

6. WEEKLY REPORT

7. NEXT GENERATION SAMPLE ITINERARY

1.

SAMPLE NEW CLIENT LOG

Client Name	New Assets	Date Received	Type of Transfer	YTD	Subtotal	QTR	New Relationships	Notes
Last Name								
Last Name								
Last Name								
Last Name								
Last Name								
Last Name								
Last Name								
Last Name								
Last Name								
Last Name								
Last Name								
Last Name								
Last Name								

2.

SAMPLE NEW ASSET LOG

Client Name	New Assets	Date Received	Type of Transfer	YTD New Assets	Total New Assets	QTR	Notes	Source
Last Name				$	$			
Last Name				$	$			
Last Name				$	$			
Last Name				$	$			
Last Name				$	$			
Last Name				$	$			
Last Name				$	$			
Last Name				$	$			
Last Name				$	$			
Last Name				$	$			
Last Name				$	$			

3.

SAMPLE CLIENT LOSS LOG

Client Name	Lost Assets	Date of Loss	Type of Transfer	YTD	Subtotal	QTR	Lost Relationship	Notes
Last Name								
Last Name								
Last Name								
Last Name								
Last Name								
Last Name								
Last Name								
Last Name								
Last Name								
Last Name								
Last Name								
Last Name								

4.

SAMPLE FEE ASSETS LOG

Bruno	Assets Moved to Fee Account	Date Moved	YTD Total	Total Fee Assets	QTR	Notes
Name						
Name						
Name						
Name						
Name						
Name						
Name						
Name						
Name						
Name						
Name						
Name						

SAMPLE ASSET FLOW SUMMARY					
Net Summary	**YTD**	**Q1**	**Q2**	**Q3**	**Q4**
New Relationships					
Lost Relationships					
New Assets from New Relationships	$	$	$	$	$
New Assets from Current Relationships	$	$	$	$	$
Total New Assets	$	$	$	$	$
Total Client Losses	$	$	$	$	$
Asset Flow	$	$	$	$	$
Mortgage Fee	$	$	$	$	$
Asset Flow to Feee Based Accounts	$	$	$	$	$

New Client Assests Summary	**YTD**	**Q1**	**Q2**	**Q3**	**Q4**
ACAT	$	$	$	$	$
CERTIFICATE	$	$	$	$	$
CHECK	$	$	$	$	$
TRANSFER	$	$	$	$	$
WIRE	$	$	$	$	$
OTHER	$	$	$	$	$
Total	$	$	$	$	$

New Assests Summary	**YTD**	**Q1**	**Q2**	**Q3**	**Q4**
ACAT	$	$	$	$	$
CERTIFICATE	$	$	$	$	$
CHECK	$	$	$	$	$
TRANSFER	$	$	$	$	$
WIRE	$	$	$	$	$
OTHER	$	$	$	$	$
Total	$	$	$	$	$

Lost Assests Summary	**YTD**	**Q1**	**Q2**	**Q3**	**Q4**
ACAT					
CERTIFICATE					
CHECK					
TRANSFER					
WIRE					
OTHER					
Total					

5.

6.

WEEKLY REPORT						
Net Summary	YTD	Q1	Q2	Q3	Q4	AUM (Mgd) 6/21/18
New Relationships						Source
Lost Relationships						Source
New Assets from New Relationships						Source
New Assets from Current Relationships						Source
Total New Assets						Source
Total Client Losses						Source
Asset Flow						Total AUM (mgd all)
Mortgage Fee						
Asset Flow to Fee Based Accounts						

Assets - New Relationships		Lost Relationships	
Client	$	Client	$
Client	$	Client	$
Client	$	Client	$
Client	$	Client	$
Client	$	Client	$
Client	$	Client	$
Client	$	Client	$
Client	$	TOTAL	$
Client	$		
Client	$		
Client	$		
TOTAL			

Week of	to	
New Client Assets		$0
New Assests		$0
Total Assets Lost		
WTD Asset Flow		$0
Mortgage Fees		
Asset Flow to Fee Based Accounts		$0

Month to Date of	
New Client Assets	$0
New Assests	$0
Total Assets Lost	
MTD Asset Flow	$0
Mortgage Fees	
Asset Flow to Fee Based Accounts	$0

Year to Date for	
New Client Assets	$0
New Assests	$0
Total Assets Lost	
YTD Asset Flow	$0
Mortgage Fees	
Asset Flow to Fee Based Accounts	$0

NEXT GENERATION SAMPLE ITINERARY

DAY 1		
TIME	SESSION TOPIC	SPEAKER
12:15 – 1:45pm	Lunch and Overview of Firm	CEO Head of Business Development
2:00 – 2:45pm	Banking and Lending Solutions	Head of Banking & Lending Solutions Banking Products Manager
2:45 – 3:00pm	BREAK	
3:00 – 4:30pm	Family Legacy, Governance, Philanthropy	Head of Wealth Management Head of Financial Planning
4:30 – 5:30pm	Cyber Security and Identity Protection	Chief Technology Officer
6:30pm	Dinner	Client's Financial Advisor Team

7.

NEXT GENERATION SAMPLE ITINERARY

DAY 2		
TIME	**SESSION TOPIC**	**SPEAKER**
8:30 – 9:30am	Breakfast and Portfolio Implementation	Client's Financial Advisor Team
9:30 – 10:30am	FinTech Innovation, Artificial Intelligence, and Machine Learning	Executive Director, Digital Wealth Management Executive Director, Technology and Intelligent Solutions
10:30 – 12:00pm	Overview of Markets and Economics	Senior Global Economist Managing Director
12:00 – 1:45pm	Lunch	Client's Financial Advisor Team
2:45 – 3:30pm	Commercial & Investment Banking for a privately held company	Managing Director
3:30 – 4:30pm	Family succession planning for a privately held company	Managing Director Head of Wealth Management

BIBLIOGRAPHY

Backman, Maurie. "Most Americans Don't Trust Their Financial Advisors. Should They?" The Motley Fool. July 11, 2017. Accessed March 29, 2019. https://www.fool.com/retirement/2017/07/11/most-americans-dont-trust-their-financial-advisors.aspx.

Beattie, Andrew. "Market Crashes: The Dotcom Crash (2000-2002)." Investopedia. Accessed March 29, 2019. https://www.investopedia.com/features/crashes/crashes8.asp.

Egan, Matt. "Dow plunges 1,175—worst point decline in history." CNNMoney. February 5, 2018. Accessed March 29, 2019. https://money.cnn.com/2018/02/05/investing/stock-market-today-dow-jones/index.html.

Financial Times. "FT 400 Top Financial Advisers 2017 listing." March 30, 2017. Accessed March 29, 2019. https://www.ft.com/content/91ac38b8-1479-11e7-b0c1-37e417ee6c76.

Florida Trend. "JPMorgan Chase to Add 35 Branches in Florida in Next Three Years." September 27, 2018. Accessed March 29, 2019. https://www.floridatrend.com/article/25515/jpmorgan-chase-to-add-35-branches-in-florida-in-next-three-years.

Forbes. "Best-In-State Wealth Advisors." Accessed March 29, 2019. https://www.forbes.com/best-in-state-wealth-advisors/#2aedb542291d.

"Top Wealth Advisors." June 30, 2018. Accessed March 29, 2019, https://www.forbes.com/top-wealth-advisors/#5ef1c7e61a14.

Garmhausen, Steve. "Highlights From Barron's 2018 Top 1,200 Financial Advisors Ranking," *Barron's*, March 10, 2018, accessed March 29, 2019, https://www.barrons.com/articles/americas-top-1-200-financial-advisors-1520651090.

Green, Kelli A., Mayra López, Allen Wysocki, Karl Kepner, Derek Farnsworth, and Jennifer L. Clark. "Diversity in the Workplace: Benefits, Challenges, and the Required Managerial Tools." University of Florida, IFAS Extension. Revised October 2015. Accessed March 29, 2019. https://edis.ifas.ufl.edu/hr022.

Kaufman, Karl "What Does The Future Hold For Financial Advisors?" *Forbes*. August 31, 2018. March 29, 2019. https://www.forbes.com/sites/karlkaufman/2018/08/31/what-does-the-future-hold-for-financial-advisors/#1daf31907876.

KPMG. "Evolving Investment Management Regulation: Succeeding in an uncertain landscape." June 2017. Accessed March 29, 2019. https://assets.kpmg/content/dam/kpmg/za/pdf/2017/06/emir-2017.pdf.

Letzing, John. "WaMu seized, sold to J.P. Morgan Chase." MarketWatch. September 26, 2008. Accessed March 29, 2019. https://www.marketwatch.com/story/wamu-fails-sold-to-jp-morgan-chase-for-19-billion.

Low, Elaine. "Are Women Better Investors Than Men? Here's What The Studies Say." Investor's Business Daily. July 16, 2018. Accessed March 29, 2019. https://www.investors.com/news/women-investing-stocks-outperform-men-studies/.

Lynch, Peter, with John Rothchild. *One Up On Wall Street: How To Use What You Already Know To Make Money In The Market*, 2nd ed. (New York: NY: Simon & Schuster, April 3, 2000).

Malito, Alessandra. "Women are about to control a massive amount of wealth but can't find anyone to manage it." MarketWatch. May 15, 2017. Accessed March 29, 2019. https://www.marketwatch.com/story/women-are-about-to-control-a-massive-amount-of-wealth-but-cant-find-anyone-to-manage-it-2017-05-12.

Mann Jr., Joseph A. "Gateway City/Who's Here: Chase a major player in Florida banking since 2009." Business Monday, *Miami Herald*. December 17, 2015. Accessed March 29, 2019. https://www.miamiherald.com/news/business/biz-monday/article50579145.html.

Oechsli Institute with First Clearing. "Best Practices of Today's Elite Advisors." October 2015. Accessed March 29, 2019. https://www.firstclearing.com/static-media/papers/FCC_BestPractices_CAR0718-00166-ADA-LOCKED.pdf.

OppenheimerFunds & Campden Wealth Research. "Coming of Age: The Investment Behaviors of Ultra-High Net Worth Millennials in North America." 2017.

Polyak, Ilana. "For some widows, breaking up with an advisor is easy to do." CNBC. October 11, 2014. Accessed March 29, 2019. https://www.cnbc.com/2014/10/10/husbands-gone-widows-part-ways-with-advisors-too.html.

PwC United States. "Managing millennial money." Accessed March 29, 2019. https://www.pwc.com/us/en/industries/financial-services/library/managing-millennial-money.html.

Roeder, Jarrad. "The Future of Digital Financial Advice." Heidrick & Struggles, CFP Board Digital Advice Working Group. December 15, 2016. Accessed March 29, 2019. https://www.heidrick.com/Knowledge-Center/Publication/future_digital_financial_advice.

Sclafani, Ray. *You've Been Framed: How to Reframe Your Wealth Management Business* (Hoboken, NJ: Wiley, 2015).

Skinner, Liz. "The great wealth transfer is coming, putting advisors at risk." Investment News. July 13, 2015.

U.S. News & World Report. "Baby Boomer Report 2015." 2015. Accessed March 29, 2019, https://www.usnews.com/pubfiles/USNews_Market_Insights_Boomers2015.pdf.

Vries, Lloyd. "Procter & Gamble Acquires Gillette." CBS News. January 28, 2005. Accessed March 29, 2019. https://www.cbsnews.com/news/procter-gamble-acquires-gillette/.